THE LEGACY OF KATHARINE HEPBURN: FINE ART AS A WAY OF LIFE

A Memoir

By

Maryann Pasda DiEdwardo

Bloomington, IN   authorHOUSE®   Milton Keynes, UK

AuthorHouse™
1663 Liberty Drive, Suite 200
Bloomington, IN 47403
www.authorhouse.com
Phone: 1-800-839-8640

AuthorHouse™ UK Ltd.
500 Avebury Boulevard
Central Milton Keynes, MK9 2BE
www.authorhouse.co.uk
Phone: 08001974150

This book is a work of non-fiction. Unless otherwise noted, the author and the publisher make no explicit guarantees as to the accuracy of the information contained in this book and in some cases, names of people and places have been altered to protect their privacy.

First published by AuthorHouse   3/1/2007

ISBN: 1-4259-6089-8 (sc)

Printed in the United States of America
Bloomington, Indiana

This book is printed on acid-free paper.

"I can remember walking as a child. It was not customary to say you were fatigued. It was customary to complete the goal of the expedition."

Katharine Hepburn (Anderson 90).

It is not the fashion to see the lady the epilogue; but it is no more unhandsome than to see the lord the prologue.

(Rosalind, <u>As You Like It</u>, Act V. Epilogue).

The legacy of the late Katharine Hepburn undeniably benefits a twenty-first century audience, because Kate identifies the artistic spirit that spans societal limitations and cultural attributes. As one of the most important women of the twentieth century, Hepburn was an artist who exemplified the independent character, freedom and opportunity available to women as paramount whether she was on stage or in film. As the late Hepburn, she has become a living art spirit with a legacy that acts as a shining example.

In contrast to reviews of past two twenty-first century performances, we can surmise that in the early part of the twentieth century, the staging and acting devoted itself to the beauty of the Forest of Arden and the majestic performance of Rosalind as paramount to the production. Katharine Hepburn lived up the challenge and played the heroine as paramount to the production with her charm and wit as a force for audiences to enjoy.

DEDICATION

Dedicated to two women and one man who helped to shape my tapestry study that encapsulates my visions for a future that is bright and filled with fine art for all humans:

To my mother, J.D. Pasda, who encouraged me from conception to be all that I could be. J.D. inspired me to write this book based on her meeting with Katharine Hepburn after a performance of Rosalind at the Cort Theatre in New York City. As a young woman, J.D. found Hepburn still in costume; the dignified actress shook my mother's hand. With admiration for Kate's graciousness, J.D. realized that her talent was one of sheer greatness that would weather the tests of time and provide a true legacy for future women in performing art.

To the late Katharine Hepburn, actress, painter, writer, speaker, and model for the performing artist way of life, a branch of fine art, for her "unsurpassed dramatic strength" as the description from the trailer for Dragon Seed would deem her. J.D. comments that Hepburn portrayed women with strength to create a specific voice for characters to carry the role and step further than others. I envision the voice of Hepburn to be alive in this book to speak to future generations through a weaving of research and personal reflections on the works and purposeful commitment to study of performing art as a way of life, future educational paradigm, and functional theory of being well during life on earth.

To the late Professor Frank Hook, former Head of the Lehigh University English Department, Bethlehem, Pennsylvania, an educational scholar who allowed me to be myself while studying formal English Literature. He encouraged my interest in the possibility of stage history as a viable academic subject to approach a thesis as well as to approach my life's work. Thank you Frank and all educators who give students like me a chance to try.

From all three I have learned persistence, vision, and courage.

ACKNOWLEDGEMENT

I thank Pam of Authorhouse for her inspiration and confidence.

CONTENTS

COVER ILLUSTRATION

Katharine Hepburn as Rosalind in the production of As You Like It directed by Michael Benthall for The Theatre Guild at the Cort Theatre in New York City in 1950

ABSTRACT

William Shakespeare created Rosalind in the pastoral comedy *As You Like It* which as first performed on December 2, 1603. In this investigative study, I have provided a discussion and analysis of the performances of three actresses who portrayed Rosalind in the twentieth century. Edith Evans played Rosalind in productions of As You Like It at the Old Vic Theatre in London England in 1926 under that direction of Andrew Leigh, and again in 1937 directed by Esme Church; Katharine Hepburn portrayed the heroine at the Cort Theatre in New York City in 1950 directed by Michael Benthall, and Vanessa Redgrave created the role at the Aldwych Theatre in London, England in 1961 directed by Michael Elliott. Four conclusions concerning methods of producing As You Like It and interpretations of Rosalind in the twentieth century emerge from this study: (1) methods of theatrical production changed between 1926 and 1961 as illustrated by the comparison of four productions of As You Like It; (2) Esme Church directed the most outstanding production of As You Like It; (3) though Edith Evans, Katharine Hepburn and Vanessa Redgrave approached the role with similar acting techniques, they interpreted Rosalind differently; (4) Edith Evans gave the most successful performance of Rosalind.

PROLOGUE

I welcome the reader to a performance of twenty five
years produced by myself and William Shakespeare

The Legacy of Katharine Hepburn, A Tribute To Fine Art As A
Way of Life.

All the world's a stage,

And all the men and women merely players:

They have their exits and their entrances;

And one man in his time plays many parts,

His acts being seven stages. At first the infant,

Mewling and puking in the nurse's arms.

Then the whining school-boy, with his satchel

And shining morning face, creeping like snail

Unwillingly to school. And then the lover,

Sighing like furnace, with a woeful ballad

Made to his mistress' eyebrow. Then a soldier,

Full of strange oaths, and bearded like the pard,

Jealous in honour, sudden and quick in quarrel,

Seeking the bubble reputation

Even in the cannon's mouth. And then the justice,

In fair round belly with good capon lined,

With eyes severe and beard of formal cut,

Full of wise saws and modern instances;

And so he plays his part. The sixth age shifts

Into the lean and slipper'd pantaloon,

With spectacles on nose and pouch on side,

His youthful hose, well saved, a world too wide

For his shrunk shank; and his big manly voice,

Turning again toward childish treble, pipes

And whistles I his sound. Last scene of all,

That ends this strange eventful history,

Is second childishness and mere oblivion,

Sans teeth, sans eyes, sans taste, sans everything.

(Jaques, <u>As You Like It</u> *Act II scene vii)*

In a personal interview with Katharine Hepburn one week before opening performance of the production in Cleveland, William F. McDermott questioned her about her approach to the role (McDermott 1950, Sect. 2, p.1, Col. 3). She revealed her interpretation of Rosalind in her answers. She said:

As You Like It is all dreaming and hoping, wonder and magic. It reminds me of when I first went to New York to try my fortune. I was so happy and so wild with excitement that my feet never touched the pavement….I am getting some of the same kind of pleasure out of trying As You Like It. The Kids like this play….We play it for romance – pure, idealized, fabulous romance.

I studied for six months three hours a day under the tutelage of Constance Collier…and developed more breath, range and color of voice.

I don't want to be bumptious (As Rosalind)….There is no thigh-slapping no athletics, no leaping (Katharine Hepburn)

One important purpose of my new work is to analyze my own conclusions from the original thesis to update the work and show how Miss Hepburn was a unique actress who took responsibility for her parts and her own career. For example, in Chapter Two, I show that her performance in As You Like It was a historical success for her own career but not a success in the comparison to other actresses of the time who played the part.

From Chapter Two Original Thesis:

Katharine Hepburn's one-sided portrayal was a result of her own personal interpretation of the role, Mr. Benthall's strict direction and Mr. Bailey's dominant scenery and costumes. These factors deterred her from developing into a more truthful Rosalind. The major problem with this production of As You Like It seemed to be the fault of the producers representing the Theatre Guild. Theresa Helburn and Lawrence Langner, production supervisors, were interested in the audience attraction of Miss Hepburn. They exploited her career to promote their organization. They shipped Mr. Benthall from England to make an impression on American audiences that the Theatre Guild's presentation of As You

Like It would be a quality production because they employed a British director. So the flaw with this production was that it was produced to bring the Theatre Guild commercial success. The director, actress and crew did not work together as one unit. Although Miss Hepburn involved herself in every aspect of the production, her assistance was not sufficient to unify the efforts of the cast and crew.

An analysis of dramatic art applies to all aspects of the production and clearly formulates a doctrine or paradigm for education of students in stage history. My new chapters extend to applications of my stage history study under Frank Hook to broaden college degrees to include works such as mine for classes and degrees. The Legacy of Katharine Hepburn, A Tribute To Fine Art As A Way of Life coordinates research by the author in partial fulfillment of the Master of Arts Degree at Lehigh University, refers to the past accomplishments of the late great actress Katharine Hepburn, recounts the life of the author as she pursues the study of fine arts in order to follow in the steps of the late Hepburn, offers a new paradigm for the study of stage history as an academic subject, lists research libraries and online resources, and paves a new method for education of the masses. Interestingly, the speech by Jacques acts as an outline for the legacy defined in this work as our remembrances, recollections, as well as applications of past accomplishments of the great actress Katharine Hepburn which are recounted with added personal anecdotes to create a new work that stimulates the reader to action based on following the legacy for future generations.

And all the men and women merely players:

The idea behind this project was to leave a legacy of hope. Our path toward greatness lies within our commitment to the education of our children. Fine art, including theatre arts, dance, music, writing, film, photography and music would be excellent methods to use in classrooms to teach young people to grow and prosper. I believe that the performing arts career of Hepburn and the stage history that accompanies that career are paramount to the understanding of a new type of educational system that can improve, synthesize a new educational system, and consequently fix our schools and our children.

We must survive as a species based on our functioning educational views to raise human beings who can act in accordance with principles. These are clearly a part of the fine arts. We can learn from one woman and use her life as a paradigm for this new educational system. We had the chance to watch her grow up in film and stage, to live, and to die. Katharine Hepburn truly was a legend for all humans to follow to find a life of fulfill through fine art. Throughout the text, I have strewn lines from the play As You Like It by William Shakespeare to retain the flavor of the original idea behind this work.

So, the main purpose of this book: promotion of fine art as a way of life, suggests dynamic change to our educational system by basing all learning on fine art: visual art, drama, dance, music, writing, film and photography. Shakespeare, whose works are so much like us, inspires the reader and adds unity to my work. Shakespeare's words resound world wide in schools, homes, churches and mosques as the most multicultural writer of all since his works were so human. Therefore, I add Shakespeare as a legacy builder to my work and breathe life into the book via remembering Katharine Hepburn and suggesting a new wave of educational theory based on fine art as a door to the mind of humans. We can learn from her joy of life by imitating her performing art skills and applying them to any profession. Development of the body through exercise, presentation of speech skills, networking in a global economy, are all types of strategies that fine artists offer as a basis for formation of life skills for youth. So I create a tapestry as I combine Katharine Hepburn's legacy with a basic pattern designed to reflect the unity in Shakespeare's As You Like It by use of quotations and story line references that mirror Hepburn's legacy, educational theory, research possibilities, a new educational paradigm and lessons for students of all ages. In actuality, I have created a work that is usable for twentieth century folks, scholars, audiences, Shakespearean fans, and scholars as well as educators and students who seek to know the reasons why Hepburn was such as famous actress and why her past accomplishments are so very important for future generations.

The drama of <u>The Legacy of Katharine Hepburn, A Tribute To Fine Art As A Way of Life</u> delights, entertains, and demonstrates stage history at its finest: stage history to honor a great actress. I have chosen to honor the late Katharine Hepburn since she has been my mentor for my entire life. Ever since I can remember, I was watching her movies or talking about her private life. She was a shadow over my life that guided me and nurtured me in the strategies of how to live and will show me eventually how to die. I decided to write about her for my Master's Thesis; again I write about her for an internationally published book as I have held on to my perceptions of Katharine Hepburn: a light in my path that guides my artistic spirit to continue to grow.

The work is not a biography but in a sense an art spirit journey based on the author's previous work and expanded to present a new educational paradigm for educators as well as a vision of the artistry of Hepburn as representational of feminism and of highest female dramatic art of a culture. Her portrayal of the beautiful Rosalind a witty daughter of a banished Duke began my quest to find out why Hepburn made and will make such an impact on fine art as a way of life with her ability to perform through decades and grow old within theatre art world.

The artistry of Hepburn lies within her talent for developing a life devoted to the fine arts of acting and painting. I suggest that her quest for a life style in drama and eventually in art as a past time enriched her life and allowed her to be happy in the midst of the tensions of career and personal intrigue of love and family. I intend to analyze the need for stage history in our current educational setting and expound on the virtues of fine art as an opening into the human brain that melds all wounds and allows humans to find ways to cope with life's dilemmas. I have used my Doctoral Dissertation empirical research where I identified the relationship between the use of modern music and teaching English in the college classroom to extend my theories that theatrical art, drama and art can create a better human being or a happier one who can achieve more in life due to expansion of the right side of the brain. In the dissertation, I found that modern music in the college English classroom transformed the classroom and allowed the student to learn literature, writing, and computer skills through the theory that promoted coparticipation precedes the knowledge (Mary Catherine Bateson, 1975).

Music transformed the college student's mind and prepared the student to learn. The participation in the listening of music and the selection of favorite music by the student prepared the student to learn about literature, writing, and computer skills appropriate for writing.

I learned that stage history can be a viable academic subject and I intend to promote that for the rest of my life. The struggle to write a stage history thesis began in 1979 when I suggested the topic to Professor Frank Hook. He allowed me to try. I thank him and find that the moment of truth and tribute of Kate began with the first step in the study process when I decided to visit New York City and find stage history reviews. This therefore I site as the basis of this work. I want the reader to set up goals and achieve the answers to questions that linger in the subconscious that are intuitive insights into the brain. Listen to your own mind and follow your ideas. I did and I find the role model of Hepburn as a life quest to be inspiring and usable. Her art acting, social, personal and female qualities all shine out as part of her legacy.

Initially, I ask the reader to explore my findings in my study; then, I wander into new paths and explore my lessons in drama as well as my hope that stage history will become a viable major in academic settings and will even be added to early childhood elementary and secondary curriculums. My basic argument lies in knowledge I gained from activity in drama for forty five years and participation in the fine arts for fifty years. I learned to paint at the age of one in the kitchen. I learned to act at the age of two when I would write and act out my own plays. I learned to sing, dance, play piano as well. So, the thesis leads me to a new wave for our children and our educational system.

My paradigm uses the legacy of Hepburn and sets up study patterns that develop the whole person.

I added the following additional sections to enhance the document:

> Chapter Four Katharine Hepburn with filmography, theatre and television appearances and short biography, Chapter Five with thesis appendix lists expanded and updated, Chapter Six on the importance of stage history in the twenty-first century to extend knowledge of the promotion of stage history as a viable academic subject, list how to become a stage historian, where to study, as well as how to write works in formatted lessons for stage history enthusiasts with current theories about the subject and review of current and past scholars; Chapter Seven covers a list of stage history via online facilities.

The history of the document is important to Lehigh University where I consider myself a part of the Lehigh family. Most of the data from this work originates with my personal journals which I started to keep in 1960. As I have always wanted to write, a young playwright at the age of three, I noted any influences that came my way such as the performances of Hepburn that intrigued me. The original idea for this project was conceived at the kitchen table during a conversation with my mother, artist and writer, J.D. Pasda. She explained that I might use my interest in Shakespeare to write a thesis for my Master of Arts in English at Lehigh University and provided an original playbill for a performance of <u>As You Like It</u> with Katharine Hepburn starring as the lead role of Rosalind in <u>As You Like It</u> at the Cort Theater in New York City. Josephine attended the performance and told me the performance of Katharine Hepburn was an exuberant, life changing experience.

The idea intrigued me: a performance that could change a life. The idea that stage history could be a viable academic subject and a respected thesis subject at Lehigh University has been a focus for me in my personal journals for twenty four years since I graduated from Lehigh University. My thesis demonstrated the use of stage history to write and study Shakespeare. In this endeavor, the review became the master research document and the collection of reviews demonstrates the use of culture to teach how the literature comes alive on stage. In a sense, the review becomes the scholarly document to record the performance for all time. Ultimately, the document intertwined with the knowledge of J.D., my mother, about Hepburn's career. My mom had a lively memory that is implemented in this work. She was an avid theatre goer and also loved Hepburn. Notes from her memoirs have helped me formulate Chapter Four.

Once we established that reviews would suffice as background research with visits to libraries via mail and travel, my advisor Barbara Traister and the Head of the English Department, Frank Hook, helped me design a project entitled: "Rosalind in the Twentieth Century: An Analysis of Performances by Edith Evans, Katharine Hepburn and Vanessa Redgrave." The work is here in a revised form as a book and will be dedicated to Lehigh Professor Frank Hook and Katharine Hepburn with three chapters expanded to seven chapters. In 1979-80, under the editing guidance of Lehigh University Professor Barbara Traister, I obtained approval, planned the two year project, and created a work based on research from New York and London through the privilege of working with the late Professor Frank Hook. Most importantly, I honor the work of Frank Hook in his teaching at Lehigh University; I dedicated the book to him. Frank gave me time to search for appropriate data that I eventually found in reviews, playbills, and theatrical libraries all of which are listed in my book.

The original unpublished work entitled "Rosalind in the Twentieth Century: An Analysis of Performances by Edith Evans, Katharine Hepburn and Vanessa Redgrave" manuscript of three chapters is approximately 20,000 words with five photos in black and white. In addition, the document contained an eight page bibliography, and six appendix sections with cast lists and list of libraries and centers for performing arts research in the United States and England. Conclusively, stage history is a marvelous topic for Lehigh University at this time when Lehigh is moving toward an arts centered curriculum. My book is current both due to my popularity in our local community and in our Lehigh family and the opportunity for global readers and researchers to apply my educational paradigm for use of stage history as a new field for academic scholarship vital to 21st century study.

On the sojourn of life, I often find that being an artist defines me. Katharine Hepburn, her career and personal life mirror my life and the lives of all female artists and writers who seek command over a changing society view of women. Her artistry defined her personal life. In fact, she wrote me a letter in reference to my Master's Thesis for Lehigh University in 1979 to let me know that she did not grant personal interviews at that time, but that I could find data on her performance of Rosalind in New York City at the Library of the Performing Arts at Lincoln Center. In that simple but elegant document, I have found strength and courage to pursue my life as a research effort and to never give up if the research seems impossible. Subsequently, this persistence has lead me to create careers in writing, art, and scholarship that continue.

Katharine Hepburn's energy was formidable. This current work is a legacy collection of data that will prove that stage history is viable academic subject and that Katharine Hepburn's reliance on her own personality on stage was weak as a dramatic mode in the twentieth century vision of acting but remains strong as a legacy for women of the twenty-first century. It is also the story of how Katharine Hepburn influences my life, to select research efforts based on personal skills to enhance careers, and most importantly to demonstrate that the late Hepburn is a model for the new century: strength of character and wit develops meaningful careers out of the home for men and women to redefine their educations and their lives.

Conclusively, this work is not a biography of Hepburn's life facts but a legacy based on this writer's use of Hepburn's art spirit to develop as a woman. Hepburn is and will always be a leader in the feminist movement to make women's lives better. The legacy of Katharine Hepburn shows a love of family and artistry. I have patterned my life after the legacy, and I encourage my readers to do the same. I list the ways to develop family and career paths based on fine art education within revised chapters to allow readers to note that my previous research has lead me to new ideas and thoughts based on old research. Application of stage history research to focus on life skills defines a new educational paradigm.

INTRODUCTION

William Shakespeare created his most enchanting comic heroine in the pastoral comedy, <u>As You Like It.</u> Rosalind is a creature of impulse who speaks her thoughts as they come to her. She is alternately sad and merry, despairing and confident, and the actress who plays her must reflect her moods in her face and voice with quick honest transitions. Rosalind is the primary focus of this discussion and analysis of the performances of three actresses who played her. Dame Edith Evans played Rosalind in productions of As You Like It at the Old Vic Theatre in London, England in 1926 and again in 1937; Katharine Hepburn portrayed Rosalind at the Cort Theatre in New York City in 1950, and Vanessa Redgrave created the role at the Aldwych Theatre in London, England in 1961. In the introduction to this study, I have provided a short plot synopsis and a brief stage history of <u>As You Like It,</u> as well as the reasons for my selection of two English actresses and one American actress.

The study is in three parts: (1) factual information concerning each performance; (2) a comparison of the actresses' techniques and interpretations of Rosalind and the degree of successes of all three performances; (3) an evaluative essay suggesting that Edith Evans gave the most outstanding performance. This study will demonstrate that all aspects of dramatic art must work together to make a production successful. As I attempt to recreate each performance, I will depend on the reader's imagination to envision the production. The most important goal of this study is to explore the character of Rosalind as Shakespeare created her, through the examination of three different performances by three actresses. Through an understanding of their portrayals of Rosalind, we should come to understand her and the world of Shakespeare's pastoral comedy.

William Shakespeare based <u>As You Like It</u> (c. 1599-1600) on Thomas Lodge's <u>Rosalynde</u> (pub. 1590), replete with the conventions of pastoral romance (Gassner and Quinn, 643). These conventions implied that urban life is corrupt and only in the pastoral scene could the most satisfying life, which is at once the simplest and noblest, be led. Shakespeare presented both the ideal and the real in <u>As You Like It</u> in startling juxtaposition.

The story is set in the Forest of Arden in medieval France. Before the play begins, the Duke of Burgundy had been deposed by his younger brother, Frederick. Driven from his dominions, Duke Senior fled with his faithful followers to the Forest of Arden. There he lived a happy life, free from the cares of the court and able to devote himself to learning the lessons of nature. His daughter Rosalind, however, remained at court as a companion to her cousin, Celia, the usurping Duke Frederick's daughter.

The action of the play begins as the characters who live in court prepare for a wrestling match between the Duke's champion, Charles, and a young man named Orlando, the special object of Duke Frederick's hatred. Orlando was the son of Sir Rowland de Boys, who in his lifetime had been one of the banished Duke's most loyal supporters. When Sir Rowland died, he had charged his oldest son, Oliver, with the task of looking after his father's charge. Rosalind hears of the wrestling match and tries to dissuade Orlando from what the Duke has told her is an unequal match. She fails, and sees him win the bout; afterwards she discovers that he is Sir Rowland's son (I. ii.).

Arbitrarily, Duke Frederick orders her to leave court within ten days; Rosalind, Celia, and hew faithful Touchstone, the false Duke's jester, set out for the Forest of Arden. They travel in disguise, Rosalind as a man, Ganymede; and Celia as his sister, Aliena. When they reach the forest, they buy a cottage, pasture, and flocks with the help of Corin, an old shepherd (II. iv.). Meanwhile, Orlando also fled to the Forest of Arden because of his brother's harsh treatment. He was accompanied by his faithful servant, Adam. Rosalind is astonished to find verses addressed to her hanging on trees and her name carved on their trunks. Celia tells her that the verses were written by Orlando. Rosalind, who is in love with Orlando, decides to remain disguised as Ganymede, and meets with Orlando, who does not recognize her. Rosalind tells the lovesick Orlando to meet "him" at "his" cottage for a remedy for Orlando's illness (III. ii.). Rosalind is annoyed when he does not come, and Celia doubts his constancy. As Ganymede, Rosalind interrupts Silvius' wooing of Phebe, and reproaches the shepherdess for being so bitter and scornful to her lover. Phebe falls in love with Ganymede/Rosalind (III. v.). The disguised Rosalind banters with Orlando when he arrives late, but when he has gone admits to Celia how "many fathom deep I am in love!" (IV. i.). Orlando's brother Oliver suddenly arrives bearing word to Rosalind that Orlando has been wounded rescuing him from a lioness. Rosalind faints when Oliver produces a "bloody napkin" (IV. iii.) soaked in Orlando's blood. Celia and Oliver fall in love at first meeting and planned to be married the next day. Rosalind assures Orlando that by magic art she will bring about his marriage to Rosalind at the same time. She tells Phebe and Silvius that she will resolve their love problems the next day. On that day Rosalind and Celia enter as themselves and are joyfully greeted by the Duke and Orlando; the weddings proceed.

The first performance of As You Like It was on December 2, 1603. Shakespeare's company, the King's Men, performed the play before King James at the earl of Pembroke's estate at Wilton because London theatres were closed at the time (Brown 155-156). There is no record of any revivals of As You Like It in the seventeenth century (Bates 6). Directors and producers in Europe and America found creative pleasure in producing this play during the eighteenth, nineteenth and twentieth centuries. Most retained Shakespeare's original text and characters; however, some staged so-called "improvements," re-wrote characters and experimented with staging. These "improved" productions are not the best performances of the play; they are merely quaint interpretations expressing theatrical creativity. For example, in 1723 Drury Lane stages a confused "improvement" by Charles Johnson entitled <u>Love in a Forest</u>. Johnson excised the parts of Touchstone, Phebe, Corin, William, Audrey, and Sir Oliver Martext, and dragged in bits from <u>A Midsummer Night's Dream</u>, <u>Much Ado About Nothing</u>, <u>Twelfth Night</u>, and <u>Richard III</u>. The writer also substituted a duel with rapiers for the wrestling match (Campbell 43).

Those directors who rely on Shakespeare's text produce the most successful productions of this pastoral comedy. On December 20, 1740 Charles Macklin revived the original comedy at Drury Lane, and in England it was frequently staged throughout the rest of eighteenth century. Dorothea Jordan's portrayal of Rosalind was the gay, mischievous girl that audiences expected. In America, the first performance was on July 14, 1786 at New York's John Street Theatre starring Mrs. Kenna, an able and popular actress. Before the close of the eighteenth century, <u>As You Like It</u> was played three more times in America: at the New Theatre in 1794, the John Street Theatre in 1796, and at the opening of the Park Theatre on January 29, 1798 (Speaight 71).

In the nineteenth century, <u>As You Like It</u> was popular in both England and America. Almost every notable actress played Rosalind, each bringing her own particular style of acting to the role. In fact, some established their reputations with portrayals of Rosalind. For example, when Ada Rehan appeared in Augustin Daly's American-made revival at the Lyceum in England on July 15, 1890, "Miss Rehan's Rosalind achieved for her the theatrical eminence previously attributed exclusively to Ellen Terry among Shakespearean heroines" (A Shakespearean Encyclopedia 43). Mary Anderson played the role at Stratford-on-Avon in 1885 incorporating stage business never before used in productions of <u>As You Like It</u>. She was said to have praised Orlando's verses by hugging them to her heart as she talked with Orlando himself about them (Sprague 37). On December 12, 1836, Ellen Tree chose the role of Rosalind for her American debut at the Park Theatre. "She excited enthusiastic comment, and soon afterward the part became a favorite of many popular actresses (A Shakespearean

Encyclopedia 45). Other well-known American actresses who played Rosalind during the nineteenth century were Charlotte Cushman, Mary Shaw, Fanny Wallack, Anna Cora Mowatt, Laura Keene, Louise Howard, and Julia Bennet Barrow.

Since productions of As You Like It in the twentieth century are the focus of his investigation, I have studied its stage history and changes in its production during this time both in England and America. In his book entitled Shakespearean Playgoing 1890 to 1952, Gordon Crosse suggests that productions of Shakespeare during the early part of the century could be categorized into two different styles, one called "Shakespeare Illustrated" and the other "Shakespeare Interpreted" (Crosse 89). By this distinction, Crosse explains the difference between traditional or old practices inherited from eighteenth and nineteenth century productions and the new practices of the twentieth century. The old practices placed emphasis on the star actor, cut the text often arbitrarily, and used sets which localized, pictorially, the action of the play. The new practices which evolved during the middle of the twentieth century focused on the performers as a unified company and used the original text. The stage historian Arthur Colby Sprague explains the second style, "Shakespeare Interpreted":

> ...Shakespeare's own lines conjure up backgrounds. If scenery is introduced at all, it should suggest, not represent...Scenes are no longer sharply defined but follow one another in virtually unbroken sequences...Continuity of performance is taken for attention is on essentials, on the players and the play (Sprague 152-153).

It was not until the 1930's that these practices which Sprague describes dominated Shakespearean productions in England and America. Thus, the first performance of Edith Evans in As You Like It in 1926 at the Old Vic was produced by Andrew Leigh in the old style, but her second performance in 1937 was produced by Esme Church in the new style. In the performance of Katharine Hepburn at the Cort Theatre in New York in 1950, Michael Benthall used aspects of the old and the new practices. Too much emphasis was placed on the "star" qualities of Miss Hepburn which caused other aspects of the performance to suffer. Vanessa Redgrave's performance at the Aldwych Theatre in 1961 under Michael Elliott was staged in the new style. Ironically, the new practices are similar to methods of production during Shakespeare's time. Then, "the plays of Shakespeare lived in their true medium in the care of actors on the stage" (Purdom 147). Emphasis on the interpretation of the play by the performers was important to the directors in England and America between 1937 and 1961. The degree to which a production focused on interpretation by actors rather than mere illustration largely determined the quality of the production for twentieth century critics and audience during those years.

In England a gradual change in methods of producing <u>As You Like It</u> began in the early twenties. In 1907 Oscar Ashe delivered one of his typical picture-book presentations at His Majesty's with Lily Brayton as Rosalind (Sprague 152). The stage setting controlled the production with a splendidly mounted version of the Forest of Arden. Ashe also experimented with text revisions and superfluous stage business. In 1926, Edith Evans gave a witty portrayal of Rosalind at the Old Vic under the direction of Andrew Leigh (Forbes 281-282). However, the director cut lengthy passages and the elaborate setting and costumes created realistic stage pictures but distracted the attention of the audience from Miss Evan's fine performance. Although Andrew Leigh relied on the old stage practices in 1926, hints of the new style of producing Shakespeare were apparent in earlier productions. In 1919, Nigel Playfair staged his unorthodox treatment of the comedy at Stratford. Playfair discarded traditional scenery and costumes, and even omitted the stuffed stag which since 1879 had been "religiously carried through a leaf-smothered Arden" (Purdom 26). Consequently, the producer and his cast were snubbed in the hotels and on the streets of Stratford for having dared to meddle with Shakespeare. The performers, however, were judged as giving excellent portrayals of the characters. Productions such as Playfair's lead the way for others such as that of Sir Phillip Ben Greet, who formed his own company in London in the early twenties.

His "Pastoral Players" usually performed Shakespeare outdoors. Greet broke traditional stage practice by playing without formal sets and with simply designed costumes. As a producer, Greet was noted for his ability to create a unified effort between director and actors. He did not cut the plays, carefully rehearsed transitions and speeches, and emphasized that the players must understand Shakespeare's dramatic intention (Webster 19).

In the 1937 production of <u>As You Like It</u> at the New Theatre, Esme Church incorporated the new methods of producing Shakespeare. She used a stage setting which enhanced the production but did into take away from the performers, and emphasized the acting quality of all performers of both major and minor roles. Edith Evans played a fabulous Rosalind once again. No other English actress is cited as matching her portrayal. Throughout the war, the comedy was performed almost every year. There were no London productions from 1948 until 1952 when Margaret Leighton played Rosalind at Stratford. From then on the play was staged regularly. In 1961 the best production in recent years was presented by the Royal Shakespearean Company at Stratford. Under the direction of Michael Elliott, Vanessa Redgrave created a beautiful Rosalind. Transferred to the Aldwych Theatre in 1962, the Stratford production developed to full fruition (Addenbrooke 58-59).

In America, a similar development occurred in methods of producing Shakespeare; however, American productions of <u>As You Like It</u> did not achieve the success of English productions. The Rosalinds were never considered inspired, although many performances were scenically sumptuous. Julia Marlowe played the role in American productions spanning more than twenty years, but her performances were considered inadequate. She first appeared at Tompkin's Fifth Avenue Theatre during the 1889/90 season and at the Knickerbocker Theatre in 1898. She resumed the role during a repertory season at the Academy of Music, New York, in 1910. Her husband, E. H. Sothern, portrayed Jacques in this and subsequent presentations of the comedy during the next three years, but his delivery added no new significant other character. The same has been said of Miss Marlowe's Rosalind.

Her approach to the role was too technical. She had a perfectly trained voice and a boyish gypsy quality but she did not succeed in delighting audiences with a believable performance (Speaight 84). Other actresses who played the role in America during the early part of the century were Henrietta Crosman in 1902 in New York at he Republic, Marie Booth Russell in 1911 at Daly's Theatre, Margaret Anglin in 1914 in New York at the Hudson Theatre, Edith Wynne Matthison in 1918 in New York at the Cort Theatre, and Katherin Emery in 1930 in New York at the Ritz. None of these productions were considered above mediocre (A Shakespeare Encyclopedia 46).

In 1950, Katharine Hepburn starred in a scenically gorgeous production at the Cort Theatre in New York. Michael Benthall directed this commercially successful presentation which ran for 45 performances. In 1958 the New York Shakespeare Festival offered As You Like It with Nancy Wickwire as an innocent impetuous Rosalind. Then in 1963, Joseph Papp produced an unsuccessful version of the comedy with Paula Prentiss as the comic heroine. The comedy was produced at the Stratford Festival in Ontario in 1959 and at Stratford, Connecticut in 1961. Irene Hunter played in the earlier and Kim Hunter in the later production. Both were considered adequate Rosalinds. One of the latest American efforts with the play was a musical adaptation by Dran and Tani Seitz, twin sisters who played Celia and Rosalind at the Theatre de Lys in New York. The production was considered a pleasant diversion but nothing more (A Shakespeare Encyclopedia 46).

The purpose of this investigative study is to illustrate the changes in methods of producing Shakespeare's As You Like It during the twentieth century, to study the approach of three famous Shakespearean heroines to the role of Rosalind, and to determine the reasons for the quality of each performance. I have examined what I believe are the three most outstanding performances of Rosalind given in the twentieth century: Dame Edith Evans at the Old Vic and the New Theatre in England, Katharine Hepburn at the Cort Theatre in New York City, and Vanessa Redgrave at the Aldwych Theatre in England. The productions span the period from 1926 to 1961.

The information has been obtained through newspaper and magazine reviews and articles, programs, personal letters, recordings, pictures, biographies and stage history books. Performing Arts Research Centers in the Eastern part of the United States and in England have provided valuable reviews, articles, and pictures for this study. I have provided a list of these libraries and centers for research in Appendix VI.

CHAPTER ONE

Edith Evans

Dame Edith Evans was born in Westminster, London on February 8, 1888, the daughter of post office worker Edward Evans and his wife Ellen, who ran the house as a boarding establishment. Edith became accustomed to meeting people and being at ease with them because of the numerous turnovers in boarders. Her first ambition was to be a milliner, and she apprenticed at age fifteen with a Mr. Blackaller. Some time between 1904 and 1912, Edith Evans started to attend evening classes in Shakespearean acting with Miss E.C. Massey. Miss Evans' first public performance was in October 1910 when she portrayed Viola in <u>Twelfth Night</u> produced by Roderick L. Eagle for Miss Massey's Streatham Shakespearean Players. At this performance, her extraordinary talent was noticed by producer William Poel who was responsible for transforming the young milliner into an exceptional actress. Miss Evans played a minor role under Poel's direction in 1912 in a revival of a sixth century Hindu classic called <u>Sakuntala</u> by the poet Kalidasa. In 1913, she appeared in productions at the New Royalty Theatre on Dean Street in London. "It was here that she observed, assimilated, stored experience; watching those she admired, taking from them what could best be fitted into her own personality and discarding anything that lacked truth" (Forbes). During her first season there she understudied and played a variety of characters roles. She continued her career at the Royalty through 1917, building on small roles for which more often than not she was too young. Her enthusiasm was such that she accepted everything offered gratefully and without complaint. Eventually, she played leading roles in theatres all over London. In 1921 her impersonation of Lady Utterworth in George Bernard Shaw's Heartbreak House was highly praised. She married George (Guy) Booth, a petroleum engineer, in 1924. She was then playing stock at the Old Vic. (She and her husband Booth were very close to each other though their careers often kept the apart. He was often in Venezuela. Guy Booth died 11 years after their marriage.) By 1926, Edith Evans was acclaimed as one of the few English actresses who understood and could play "the modern style of acting" (Forbes) which demanded a more realistic approach than the old style which was based on representative gestures and melodramatic line readings. Even in an affected or artificial character, she sought to find an essential truth and the simplest was of conveying it to the audience.

Edith Evans performed in over 120 plays and many films throughout her highly successful career. She won the American Film Academy Award nomination for Best Actress for her performance in The Whisperers, written for her by Bryan Forbes, and for Best Supporting Actress for her performance in Tom Jones. In 1946 she was made a Dame of the British Empire, an honor accorded to very few English actresses. She died in October 1976 in Klindown, Kent, at age 88, and is remembered as a "supreme mistress of high comedy and farce, a brilliant and versatile character actress rich in power and emotional conviction" (Skolsky).

Dame Edith Evans played Rosalind twice during her career: first in January 1926 in As You Like It at the Old Vic under the direction of Andrew Leigh; and ten years later in 1936 at the same theatre under direction of Esme Church. The second production was revived at the New Theatre in February, 1937. Miss Evans was thirty-eight when she first played Rosalind and forty-eight in her second appearance (Trewin). Both productions were acclaimed as successful. In fact, before the performance critics argued that Miss Evans was too old to play Rosalind successfully at age thirty-eight and again ten years later at age forty-eight. However, as one of her biographers points out, "arguments as to her suitability were once more demolished by her artistry" (Forbes).

The chief point of contrast between Miss Evans' two impersonations of Rosalind concerns her delivery of one line. The drama critic for the London Times who reviewed the opening of the revival on February 12, 1937 explains that Miss Evans missed a vital transition in Act IV Scene I in her performance at the New Theatre eleven years later. Rosalind, disguised as a boy, talks to Orlando about being in love in an ironic, mocking tone. Upon his exit, she turns to Celia and confesses, "O coz, coz, coz, my pretty little coz; that thou didst know how many fathoms deep I am in love!" In the 1926 performance, Edith Evans maintained her mocking attitude toward love as she spoke this line, playing up the comedy rather than allowing the audience to see the romantic side of Rosalind and her true feelings of love for Orlando; however, in the 1936 production she accomplished the subtle change of tone necessary to show the right emotion. In the performance at the New Theatre, she said this line with "passionate feeling – brilliantly and splendidly right..." effectively demonstrating her love (London Times 12). Except for her improvement upon this emotional transition, Miss Evans' performances of Rosalind in 1926 and 1936-37 were quite similar. The only other difference involves the staging by Andrew Leigh and Esme Church. Mr. Leigh used traditional costumes and settings, but Church created an experimental and adventurous staging by utilizing 18th century style costumes and setting (London Observer). Actually, this difference in staging did to affect Miss Evans' interpretation of Shakespeare's comic heroine; she created a magnificent Rosalind with superb artistic control in both performances, captivating audiences and critics alike.

Edith Evans first performed Rosalind during her opening season with the Old Vic Company, three days after her marriage to Guy Booth (Forbes). During the season from September 1925 to May 1926, Miss Evans played thirteen roles (see Appendix I), Rosalind of As You Like It being her most notable performance. According to one critic, "she produced one of the divinest pieces of comedy this astonishing actress has yet given us" (Forbes).

Although Miss Evans' performance of Rosalind was judged as "heavenly," the technical aspects of the performance are not mentioned in stage history archives. In a review of Edith Evans' portrayal of Rosalind in 1936, the critic Charles Morgan prefaces his critique with a statement that provides some insight into the 1926 production. He comments that "Ten years ago the Old Vic was a theatre chiefly devoted to usefully pious but often slightly dull productions of Shakespeare" (London Observer). Furthermore, other critics do not mention Mr. Leigh's staging of <u>As You Like It.</u> One can conjecture that in his conception of the production he did not experiment with costume, setting or stage business. During the four years when Leigh produced Shakespeare at the Old Vic (1925-29) he followed the methods of his predecessors, but did not add much innovation to his productions. Stage settings formed realistic pictures, and were quickly changed between scenes (Purdom 58). Traditional Elizabethan costumes, decorative scenery, minimal lighting and blocking typical of past productions typified Mr. Leigh's directorial process. The cast (see Appendix II) list for the 1926 production is given in a newspaper review of Edith Evans' performance of Rosalind in 1926, found in files of the Harvard Theatre Collection of the Harvard University Library. Author is identified as St. J. E. and the source of the review is called "The Week's Theatre," hereafter referred to as Harvard Theatre Collection, 1926 review. The cast performed adequately but their portrayals of Shakespeare's characters did not match Miss Evans' "wonderful performance of Rosalind" (Harvard Theatre Collection 1926 Review). Mr. Frank Vosper handsomely played Orlando "in the proper picture-book manner" (Farjeon 58). Other members of the cast who gave good performances were Mr. Balliol Holloway as Jacques and Miss Cicely Oates as Audrey. Lack of technical imagination led Mr. Leigh to depend on the talent and training of his leading lady to carry the performance. Edith Evans fulfilled these requirements so well that audiences were overjoyed to see her again as Rosalind in 1936, once more on the stage of the Old Vic.

In November 1936, Edith Evans played Rosalind at the Old Vic in a production of <u>As You Like It</u> directed by Esme Church. In the spring of 1937 the production was revived at the New Theatre for a short run. Edith Evans wrought such magic in her creation of Rosalind that, as critic Alan Dent put it, "in the end the audience was made one with Orlando. People still remember the lilt of her voice and twenty years after will quote the special emphasis and inflection she gave to a phrase (Speaight 153). Critics of this performance mutually conclude that: (1) Edith Evans portrayed the best Rosalind even seen on the English stage; (2) Mr. Michael Redgrave as Orlando gave a forthright romantic performance which complimented Miss Evans' powerful Rosalind; and (3) Molly MacArthur's Watteau style costumes and setting added a welcome change to a much over-done Shakespearean comedy. Antoine Watteau (1684-1721) was a French painter of Flemish origin who was celebrated for the lyric quality of his gay and sensuous scenes of open-air festivities. Information concerning the 1936-37 production was obtained from the following sources: reviews in New York Times, London Observer, Herald Tribune, Plays and Players, Play Pictorial, articles filed in the Harvard University Theatre Collection and the works of Bryan Forbes and J.C.Trewin.

Edith Evans' Rosalind was called clever, gay, and created with such power that she did "not merely play Shakespeare, she fulfils him" (Review of the 1937 production found in Harvard Theatre Collection entitled "As You Like It" source unknown, catalogued under Evans as Rosalind, hereafter referred to as "As You Like It" 1937.) She played the role with the control of the mannered style needed to be the lovely heroine dressed in eighteenth century silks and brocades. Edith Evans accomplished the difficult task of suing the affections of eighteenth century style costumes, setting and manners skillfully and gaily to bewitch the audience into believing that she was fathoms deep in love. She seemed to be the natural inhabitant of Arden "on a French canvas of the eighteenth century" (Brown). In fact, Miss Evans' performance was so outstanding that although Rosalind seemed to be "lingering in the Restoration" (Trewin 76) because of the Watteau setting and costumes, every line was caressed and every speech tingled. Vocally she excelled. No other actress could have danced up and down the scale on "Alas the day! What shall I do with my doublet and hose?" In her boy blue coat and breeches, she was truly Rosalind. Not only did she authentically love, but she was "the center about which all things moved. The audience was delighted, and with reason...within all the dazzle of her pretences, there was a girl in love" ("As You Like It" The London Times). Edith Evans played Rosalind with the technical brilliance of a seasoned actress, giving the part an ironic edge that was her own. Her acting had such "warmth and amplitude that she took the verse in her mind's stride and fondled it;...her way with the epilogue should become historical" ("As You Like It" The London Times). She stood next to a ten foot statue of cupid which was draped with a string of fresh flowers, and she gazed out into the audience as she fondled the flowers. Her hair was pulled back into a loosely finished bun. As she spoke, she barely moved, and delivered the final message with such care and romanticism that when she was through the audience burst into applause admiring her Rosalind.

Miss Esme Church directed the production with a mannered agreeable smoothness. She blocked the scenes with freedom and agility, allowing Miss Evans to roll around on the floor and pose against a set decoration. Directorially, she designed the play based on eighteenth century style and manner. She over-emphasized the comic scenes, playing up the wit of Rosalind. She had Edith Evans mock and glitter and play the fool with marvelous ease and grace. Her cast was well chosen (see Appendix II). Much of Miss Evans' great success with the authenticity of Rosalind's love was made possible by Mr. Michael Redgrave's Orlando which was even more romantic than Miss Evans' Rosalind. "Their playing together as Rosalind and Orlando was one of those rare marriages of professional talent and private affection that... illuminate the lives of those who perform and those who watch" (Forbes 183-184). The pair worked together closely with Miss Church, and their mutual trust, love, and understanding of the characters seems to be the major reason for the production's huge success. As a director,

Esme Church was interested in the acting quality of her entire cast, and stressed an understanding of the script. She was one of the directors in the early twentieth century to create the modern stage practices based on Shakespeare interpreted. Unlike Andrew Leigh, the director of Edith Evans' 1926 performance, Esme Church strove for a unified production where the director, technical crew and the company of performers evolved as a unified troupe.

Esme Church's success was caused in part by her close relationship not only with her cast but also with her set and costume designer, Molly MacArthur. Together, they designed a set which included a swing whose garlanded ropes apparently descended from the sky, the offstage sounds of birds, streams and summer woods, a backdrop depicting a Watteau forest in brilliant greens and blues, with arching boughs, vague silvery distances, and ornamental waters. Although one critic commented that the fancy extras of the set design were superficial ornaments which did not do anything except provide an "un-stereotyped" (Morgan) version of the forest of Arden others agree that the eighteenth century formalism...had a rate decorative charm" (The London Times). Molly MacArthur not only created a set design which provided the perfect addition to Miss Evans' high comedy and wit, but also dressed the characters in costumes which were elegant and gay. All the costumes were done in black and white. Miss Evans' dresses were made of white and silk brocade, and her blue boy style outfit was black silk with white lace. Technically, the production was as outstanding to observe as was Miss Evans' Rosalind. It is still one of the most memorable productions of <u>As You Like It</u> in the history of the play.

Katharine Hepburn

Katharine Houghton Hepburn, known as Kate, was born in Hartford, Connecticut, on November 8, 1909 (Carey and Higham). She was named after her mother who was a Boston Houghton, one of New England's wealthiest families. Her father, Dr. Thomas Norval

Hepburn, was a distinguished surgeon on the staff of the Hartford Hospital and a highly successful investor who became rich from inspired buying and selling of stock. Miss Hepburn's elder brother, Tom, and younger siblings, Dick, Bob, Marion and Peggy were all raised to practice free speech; "as soon as they could talk, they were urged to express themselves on every conceivable subject, arguing a point of view until everyone was exhausted (Higham 2)." Up to the age of ten, the actress was an uncomplicated, open-faced, freckled tomboy. But then she experienced the death of her older brother, Tom, a tragedy which "altered her character overnight, and made her, for many years, a violent antagonist of the world (Higham 5)." On Easter of 1920 she and Tom visited friends in Boston. On Saturday night after a late party, she found Tom hanging from a beam in the attic with a noose around his neck. Her agony over his death was so extreme that she became a highly nervous, moody girl, suspicious of people, arrogant and disrespectful, bitter and hating religion. At thirteen her desire to become a movie actress emerged. At that time, Katharine Hepburn appeared in <u>Marley's Ghost</u> and <u>Bluebeard</u> in a special benefit for Navajo Indian Children at Fenwick. At sixteen, she entered Bryn Mawr, her mother's alma mater, a fresh faced freckled dynamo who hated studies but fought hard to improve her grades so she could appear in college theatricals. She performed in an angular, mannered style, appearing in A.A. Milne's <u>The Truth about Blayds</u> and <u>Cradle Song.</u> In the spring of her senior year, she played a marvelous Pandora in John Lyly's <u>The Woman in the Moone</u>, earning a burst of applause from both parents and students; she decided at that moment to make definite plans for a theatrical career.

Miss Hepburn's first professional performance was in 1927 with a stock company in Baltimore under Edwin H. Knopf. She played the part of a lady-in-waiting to Mary Boland in the <u>Czarina</u>. In the other productions with Knopf in which she appeared she did not succeed because she could not memorize lines and experienced stage fright. Momentarily, she decided to give up the theatre due to her failures in acting and impulsively married Ludlow Ogden Smith. She admitted that although she could read a part extremely well, she couldn't keep it. She would lose her voice, forget lines and couldn't act. She and her husband moved to New York City, but eventually broke up after three weeks. She much preferred "Luddy" when he was not physically and domestically her husband, and in fact he became her lifelong friend. She remained legally married to him for several years to deter men who might be attracted to her.

Miss Hepburn continued living in New York after her abortive marriage, studied with the drama coach Frances Robinson-Duff, appeared in plays with the Theatre Guild, and continued acting in summer stock. Her performances as Antiope in <u>The Warrior's Husband</u> at the Morosco Theatre in New York was the turning point in her early career. The stage manager of the production Phyllis Seaton commented that "the audience was amazed by Kate...She had a terrific grace...she came down a ramp of great stairs, ran onto a platform, and jumped onto the main stage...The audience responded immediately. This was a star (Higham 19)!" From that performance, Miss Hepburn earned the prestige to take a screen test for the part of the unhappy British society girl, Sydney Fairfield in a version of Clemence Dane's play <u>A Bill of Divorcement</u>. David Selznick hired her in June, 1932. The film was a success, and Kate made the picture <u>Three Came Unarmed</u> immediately. Following this, she appeared in the films <u>Christopher Strong</u>, <u>Morning Glory</u>, <u>What Price Hollywood</u> and <u>Little Women</u>. Intoxicated by her success with the last film, Katharine Hepburn at twenty-four decided to make an immediate return to the stage.

Between 1933 and 1936 she played in several unsuccessful productions such as <u>The Lake</u> and <u>Quality Street</u> on the New York stage. She returned to Hollywood in 1937 but traveled back to New York to appear in stage productions. During this period in her career Katharine Hepburn developed a long lasting relationship with the Theatre Guild in New York, through which she played in <u>The Philadelphia Story</u> and <u>Kitty Foyle.</u> In 1941 she appeared opposite Spencer Tracy in the film <u>Woman of the Year</u> for which she was nominated for best actress. She and Tracy fell in love during the shooting of the picture, but were never married. "He was not only her adored companion but also her trusted advisor (Higham 115)." They continued a long lasing affair until his death on June 10, 1967.

In the fall of 1949 Katharine Hepburn signed a contract with the Theatre Guild to appear as Rosalind in <u>As You Like It</u>. At first she was horrified with the idea of playing Shakespeare; she had never attempted it. She worked with Constance Collier to coach her in the role for three hours a day for six months. Michael Benthall was brought from England to direct. Miss Hepburn was largely responsible for the casting, costuming, set design and involved herself in every aspect of the production. She played 145 performances and was offered the role in <u>The African Queen</u> as a result of her commercial success in <u>As You Like It.</u> Audiences recognized her as Kathatine Hepburn "the Star," although her portrayal of Rosalind was not as refined as Edith Evans'. She was not skilled in playing Shakespearean comedy, but audiences did not seem to notice. "They were charmed by Miss Hepburn's magnetism and personal beauty...her legs became the talk of New York and every night there were gasps and applause when she appeared in tights" (Carey 162).

Katharine Hepburn has won eleven Academy Award nominations and three Oscars. During her career, she played Euripides, Shakespeare, Shaw, O'Neill, Williams and Albee, a far-ranging repertoire that no other American actress of her generation can match. Over the years "she has occasionally been bad but she has rarely been boring"(Carey 238). She is an actress who has the Theatre in her hold and finds joy and excitement in her craft.

At Miss Hepburn's request, the Theatre Guild arranged a week pre-Broadway tour, which was a critical and financial success. In every city, reviews expressed admiration for Katharine Hepburn's buoyancy and grace, while the public was impressed by her beautiful appearance in doublet and hose. In a newspaper review of the road performance in New Haven, Connecticut, one critic commented that the "Production has many points in favor of its acceptance, not the least of which is a fine performance by Katharine Hepburn...other attributes include beautiful physical effects, a generally excellent troupe and interesting direction" (Bone 60). {*The newspaper review of Miss Hepburn's appearance a Rosalind in New Haven, Connecticut in December 1950 was found i*n the files of the Performing Arts Research Center at Lincoln Center, New York City.} Although critics reviewed the road show favorably, when the production opened on Broadway at the Cort Theatre on January 26, 1950, New York Theatre Critics were sharply divided as to the virtues of the production. Half praised Miss Hepburn's portrayal of Rosalind, and the other half harshly judged her performance. A close analysis of those reviews who praised Miss Hepburn's performance reveals that their praise is one dimensional; they do not praise her for transforming into Rosalind. Instead, these critics praise Katharine Hepburn as strong individual who is exciting to watch. This praise is not enough to be convincing. John Chapman of the Daily News wrote that "Miss Hepburn has a nice sense of comedy and considerable skill at timing this comedy" (Chapman 369). Aside from this comment, Mr. Chapman discusses the lavish staging and interesting movement, but does not make any comment about Miss Hepburn as a Rosalind. Howard Barnes politely finds defects in the comedy and the character of Rosalind rather than embarrassing Miss Hepburn. He suggests that "Here is a comedy handsome and somewhat dull resurrection which defeats most of Miss Hepburn's efforts to give it warmth and vitality" (Barnes 369). Richard Watts of the New York Post exclaims that "her Rosalind became a characterization of sheer loveliness" (Watts 368).

Comments such as these merely congratulate, but do not describe Miss Hepburn's Rosalind. However, those critics who attempt to analyze closely the actress's portrayal of the heroine provide an insight into her performance. Mr. Robert Garland of The American Journal explains that "Miss Hepburn, her not-too-pleasant voice Constance Collierized past immediate recognition, gets better as she goes along. Her comedy in the second act is her best" (Garland 368). Brooks Atkinson of The New York Times adds that "Miss Hepburn has too sharply defined a personality for such romantic make-believe. Her acting is tight; her voice is a little hard and shallow for Shakespeare's poetry; she has to design the character too meticulously" (Atkinson 369). Katharine Hepburn's attempt to play Rosalind was just that, an attempt. The fluctuating comments of critics indicate that her acting was unbalanced; one night she was better than the other. She had to work too hard at being Rosalind, and those reviewers who describe her performance with any intelligence focus on this fact. Katharine Hepburn was Katharine Hepburn in Arden – not Rosalind. She was a star who was loved by audiences because of her reputation as an exciting new actress who created outstanding roles on film. The performance was given over sixteen ovations every time it played because of Miss Hepburn's fame, not because she played an excellent Rosalind.

Michael Benthall reverted back to the old practices of producing Shakespeare in his conception of <u>As You Like It</u>. In an honest critique of the production, Mary Crapo Hyde explains that Miss Hepburn's production is a legitimate interpretation of <u>As You Like It</u> with lavish costumes, spectacular scenery and realistic stage effects. The production was lavishly decorated with snow, smoke, woodland notes, and borrowed songs from Love's Labor Lost which as staged effects "common to the tradition of the eighteenth, nineteenth and twentieth centuries" (Hyde 55). Benthall, a top director for the Old Vic and the Stratford-on-Avon Memorial Theatre made sure that his leading lady, Miss Hepburn, was directed to speak naturally, and move gracefully as she traveled through the forest of Arden. Mr. Benthall substituted high spirits and a youthful approach for majestic gesture and the stentorian tone" (Coleman 367). To create a realistic production, Benthall created as much movement as possible; somebody was always skipping or traipsing about the stage quite prettily" (Coleman 367). All in all, his conception was of the type considered *Shakespeare illustrated*. As a director, Benthall spent less time with characterization and more time with appearances. Both Katharine Hepburn who played Rosalind and William Prince who portrayed an adequate Orlando were praised for their fine appearances in tights and their enjoyable but not excellent characterizations. Although the rest of the cast (see Appendix IV) spoke clearly, their portrayals were considered sufficient but not exciting. Cloris Leachman was an attentive Celia, Bill Owen a bright Touchstone and Aubrey Mather a fatherly Duke. Michael Benthall emphasized visual effects rather than acting quality.

Technically, the production was a tremendous success. James Bailey created realistic stage pictures with colorful backdrops of woodland settings which showed both winter and spring. He placed three trees in the woodland glade. His costuming was authentic sixteenth century garb. His doublet and hose design for Miss Hepburn was designed to show off her legs. Bailey took advantage of her physique and fitted her clothing just right. She was the most beautiful Ganymede ever seen in Arden. For the feminine costumes Bailey used traditional Elizabethan costume: a bodice which is tight, flat across the chest, long-waisted, with a pointed front, a corset, an undergown, puffy sleeves, white neck-ruff, and a simple slipper (Barton 224). The male attire was also authentic and handsomely done. Bailey's sets and costumes made the forest of Arden "the place of idyllic enchantment" (Watts 368) for both the players and the audience. Incidental music was played by a full chamber orchestra conducted by Robert Ivring, and Frank Rogier sang Shakespearean songs periodically throughout the performance. Technically, the production captured the essential elements of make believe (Theatre Arts Monthly 14).

Vanessa Redgrave

Vanessa Redgrave, born on January 30, 1937 in London, England, was raised in a theatrical home with three generations of players. Her father, Michael Redgrave, played Orlando opposite Edith Evans' Rosalind the same year Vanessa was born. The evening of the day of her birth Michael Redgrave was playing Laertes and Sir Lawrence Olivier was playing Hamlet. Before the curtain was drawn, Olivier announced: "Today a lovely actress was born" (Goodwin 47). This story is important to Vanessa Redgrave because it suggests the love for theatre which she inherited. But this natural gift or attraction to the theatre did not make her a natural actress; her early photographs show a reticent, thoughtful child, awkwardly tall for the stage. As a child Miss Redgrave and her brother would improvise stories and characters, and since there was a profession in which "you could go on doing this" (Goodwin 168) she decided to formally study acting. In her early teens she began formal study at the Central School of Speech and Drama. At that point she was very awkward, self-conscious of her height (she is nearly six feet tall) and spoke with a raspy tone. However, she studied speech elocution and learned the Stanislavsky Acting Technique which she valued and tried to master in the minor parts she played during the ensuing years. She played minor roles in repertory at Frinton-on-Sea, and in West End productions. In these productions she learned to manipulate her contralto voice, overcome her height, move gracefully and naturally on stage and relax in front of the audience (New York Times). In her early years of theatre experience, the actress was fascinated by ballet and modern dance which she studied intensely. In her acting career Miss Redgrave relies on dance to control her movements. The discipline of dancing made her aware that every gesture and turn of the head is vital and must be controlled by the actress on stage.

Vanessa Redgrave played Valeria in Coriolanus and Helena in A Midsummer Night's Dream for the Royal Shakespeare Company in 1959. She established her potential as an actress in 1961 in her portrayal of Rosalind in As You Like It for the Royal Shakespearean Company at the Aldwych Theatre (New York Times). At twenty-four she was acclaimed by critics as an actress who was miraculously endowed with the gift of being and giving herself on stage. In a newspaper review for the London Observer Irving Wardle explains her Rosalind as "radiant." He says "it glows from within and it illuminates the rest of the stage...Miss Redgrave now owns this part, and it will be a long time before anyone else can touch it without coming under her shadow" (R.M.B.). Vanessa Redgrave is considered the loveliest Rosalind since Edith Evans. One reviewer comments that "If there is a comparison between Miss Evans and Miss Redgrave, the two leading Rosalinds of the last half-century, it is that of gold and silver" ("A Rosalind We Shall Always Remember"). Miss Redgrave's next notable performance was as Nina in Chekhov's The Seagull. Reviewers praised her a technically intelligent actress who was able to place the character in her situation and society with believable emotion. Vanessa Redgrave has played in films and television serials in addition to the stage. In The Prime of Miss Jean Brodie she fully developed her saving comic intelligence which has given her acting style its own peculiar magic. She can bring to life the beauty of Shakespeare and the emotion of Tennyson. She is famous for her portrayal of Leonie in the film Morgan, A Suitable Case for Treatment in 1965; Jane in the film Blow Up in 1966; and Isadora in the film Isadora Duncan in 1968. In addition to her film career, she has performed for the Royal Shakespearean Company throughout her career, one of her most famous portrayals being Katharina in The Taming of the Shrew in 1962.

Vanessa Redgrave is known as a bold individual who uses her acting career for political ends. She became involved with the Committee 100, a political organization in England at the same time she was playing Rosalind in As You Like It, during her first season at Stratford. She explains that her political involvements make her more "aware of the people" (Goodwin 171) she is playing for. From 1961 on she has fought for causes she believes in: her political reputation is hated by some and admired by others. It cannot be denied that Vanessa Redgrave is a fine actress and an aggressive individualist. She presently resides in London, England.

The Royal Shakespearean Theatre presented As You Like It initially at Stratford-on-Avon in London. The production opened on July 5, 1961, then played to the end of August, and was resumed in repertory at the Aldwych Theatre in London for five months (Sammassimo letter). The British Broadcasting System made a film of the production in 1962 (Addenbrooke, "As You Like It," New York Times 1961 review, Ellis 1948, Lambert 1961 and 1962, Wardle 1962). In addition to Vanessa Redgrave's Rosalind, other aspects of the production received high praise; acting of the entire cast (Appendix IV), the ingenious direction by Michael Elliott, the simple yet creative design by Richard Negri, and the elegantly designed lighting by Richard Pilbrow. The production was said to be the only presentation of <u>As You Like It</u> which compared to the 1937 production at the Old Vic.

Vanessa Redgrave played a Rosalind "brimming with hope, heroic… lyrical" (Tynan) and most importantly with sheer honesty. "Born under a dancing star" (Speaight 282), the actress fully possessed Rosalind's special quality – that of investing what is most serious to her with the charm of an exquisite frolic. At times during the performance she showed her nervousness by a quivering lip or an awkward gesture. Miss Redgrave used her youth to create a radiant, charming, exquisitely amusing Rosalind. A reviewer for the <u>London Times</u> clearly defines her portrayal as "too ecstatically girlish in her infatuation" (<u>London Times</u> 1962). This reviewer contends that she eventually tones down this melodramatic quality and "grows in strength" and gains control of her expression of love as the play proceeds. She developed an innate elation in Rosalind which gave the character a dignity and a control on stage. Nearly six feet tall, Miss Redgrave presented a commanding Rosalind. Other cast members contributed strong support. Ian Bannen played a strong Orlando, Patrick Wymark a superb Touchstone and Max Adrien a fine melancholy Jaques.

Michael Elliott developed his production by devoting himself to the quality of each performer. Elliott emphasized cohesion in his direction, in relationships between characters and in his total production. He "split the comedy nearly down the middle so that it opened with a vein of dark reality and changed at the interval to a sunlit idyll {a transformation heavily underlined by the lighting}" (Wardle). Treating his cast as an ensemble, Mr. Elliott's superb knowledge of Shakespeare allowed him to develop the characters of Shakespeare's Arden to their full potential. The lines flowed as did the emotions. Most importantly, each production was released with a freshness. The performers were comfortable in their roles yet played with a new enthusiasm during each new performance.

The technical aspects of the production complimented the actors on stage but did not detract from or dominate the performance. Richard Negri designed the set which consisted of one tree of great girth; a few effective and shadowy backdrops transformed the simply designed set piece into Oliver's orchard, Duke Frederick's court and the Forest of Arden. Richard Pilbrow worked closely in his lighting design with Mr. Elliot to provide the correct mood to enhance the scenes on stage. Technically, the production epitomized the requirements of production Shakespeare according to the new stage practices of the twentieth century; the director, the set and lighting designer worked as one unit to give the performers mood and atmosphere in which they could transform into the characters of <u>As You Like It.</u>

CHAPTER TWO

Rosalind is a character who touches the audiences with her control over the world of Arden and the destinies of its inhabitants. She has the role of omniscient controlling force in <u>As You Like It</u>; her chief function is to bring about a synthesis of different and even conflicting attitudes to love as these are expressed in the love affairs of four pairs of lovers. Through Rosalind, Shakespeare blends the feeling of romantic love with clarity of judgment. Love in Arden's world is hers, but she is the satirist of love as well. She is in disguise for most of the play, and flaunts and enjoys the freedom it allows her. Rosalind can deploy her quick wit in disguise as Ganymede in a way that she could not do in her own person. She mocks Orlando at the same time as she enjoys being in love with him. The audience and Rosalind have the advantage over all the other characters in the play with the first wooing scene, (III. ii.). The exploitation of the central secret of the play begins here. At the conclusion of the play, Rosalind relinquishes her control; romantic love dominates and the comic resolution takes place. There is a complexity to Rosalind's spirit because she sets the pace for the whole play. She serves Shakespeare as a comic spirit with knowledge beyond the world of Arden.

When Rosalind is played well, the audience is captivated by this woman who is the superior force in <u>As You Like It.</u> The actress playing Rosalind controls the lives of most of the other characters, as well as the emotions of the audience in her grasp. She uses her disguises to supplement her gifts. The actress who plays her must not only portray

Rosalind's "swashing and martial outside" (Webster 210) which allows her to control Arden, but also her tenderness, romanticism and ardor. Rosalind is a character of many dimensions who must be played with romantic love and pastoral humor. She ponders fortune's control of nature (I. ii. 41-42) with delight and yet with intelligence.

This paradox must be apparent in the portrayal of Rosalind. Edith Evans, Katharine Hepburn and Vanessa Redgrave used similar acting techniques to play Rosalind although the results of their techniques were very different. Each worked closely with her directors during the rehearsal period and relied on the basic elements of realistic acting known as The Stanislavsky System {Information on the Stanislavsky System is available in the following sources: Uta Hagen, Respect for Acting (New York: Macmillan, 1930); Elizabeth Reynolds Hapgood, trans. An Actor Prepares, by Constantine Stanislavsky (New York: Theatre Arts, 1936); Charles McGaw, Acting is Believing (New York: Holt, Rinehart and Winston, 1966); Constance M. Clark and Mary Elizabeth Devine, "The Stanislavsky System as a tool of Teaching Dramatic Literature," College English, 38, No. 1 (Sept. 1976), pp. 15-24.} This method requires the performer to become the character and find a sub-conscious life which fits the emotional sequence of the play. The players define the emotions of the play as separate beats or moments in which they define intentions. The performer then labels each intention with an active verb, so that s/he concentrates on the action rather than the words of the script. For example, in the first wooing scene (III. ii.) Rosalind begins her pursuit of Orlando, enjoys her role as Ganymede, and satirizes her own behavior toward love. When the actress plays this scene she must reveal a complex attitude which is composed of her desire to be a romantic lover and her mockery of everything we associate with romantic love. Rosalind expresses both attitudes simultaneously and with equal conviction. She never abandons her own romantic sentiments. When the actress prepares for this scene according to the Stanislavsky System, she would have to play the main intention as the attempt to romanticize about love in the abstract while she mocks love's characteristics. To accomplish this intention, the actress, assisted by her director, chooses movements, vocal intonations, and emotions which communicate her dual effort in the scene.

Edith Evans played the first wooing scene with the most control and ease of the three actresses in question. In fact, she created the most superb Rosalind. Following is a close analysis of each actress, her interpretation of Rosalind, and the reasons for the variation in interpretation. Since the director's role is to aid and to support the actress' transformation process, the conception of each director and the extent to which each succeeded in his relationship with the actress has been taken into account. Finally, the technical aspects of each performance are analyzed for their effects upon the actress' performance.

Dame Edith Evans

Edith Evans played Rosalind with steady animation, perfect innocence, charming impulsiveness and unfailing femininity. She combined tenderness with mischievousness and in both productions of <u>As You Like It</u> (1926 and 1937) she proved herself to be an excellent actress capable of playing all the complexities inherent in Rosalind. She literally transformed into the heroine who controls Arden. Miss Evans' acting was consistent and natural. She never showed how hard she was working to portray such a zestful character; instead, she became the character. Since Miss Evans' appearance did not naturally cast her for Rosalind; (she was not physically beautiful,) she created imaginatively with a girlish or boyish lightness and impudence. She moved like an arrow, rolled over on the ground in delight, mocked, glittered and played the fool with exquisite grace. If the boyishness or girlishness was not there it was because she rejected it in favor of a feminine guile that was her own edge to the part – "her deliberately implied and original conception of it" (London Times 1937 12). Within all the dazzle of her mockery and pretenses, there was a girl in love. She conjured the audience into doing exactly what Shakespeare's epilogue intended: enjoying a festive pastoral comedy.

Edith Evans based her acting technique on doing rather than talking, an important idea inherited from the Stanislavsky System. She is known for her Restoration Style of acting but denies that she made a conscious attempt during her training to develop that style. She defines the term style as instinctive "timing, which one only accumulates with experience" (Whittaker, New York Times, personal interview with Edith Evans age 72 concerning her acting technique, found in Performing Arts Research Library at Lincoln Center, cataloged under Edith Evans). By the time she was forty-eight, she was a master of her mannered style of acting. Her interpretation of the first wooing scene (III.ii.) is famous. She astonished audiences with the ease of her performance and her perfection of acting technique. Mr. Redgrave and Miss Evans played the scene so naturally that their love dominated the playful scene. Miss Evans' even slapped Orlando's legs. She portrayed Rosalind's love for Orlando by using her eyes and her physical movements to show her true feelings. Miss Evans also showed the control and fun that disguise allows Rosalind. She used her face and voice to mock Orlando for his romantic love as well as subtly to show the audience that she loved him. In this scene and in every other scene as well as her acting technique led her to find an essential truth in Rosalind which was the simplest way of conveying her to the audience (Sir John Gielgud 15).

Edith Evans was in control of both of her directors. In 1926, although she was playing her first season for the Old Vic, she relied on the habits she learned in her early training through William Poel, the first Shakespearean producer to insist on Shakespeare without cuts (Carroll). Miss Evans refused to speak a single word of Shakespeare without knowing what it meant. She believed that life had to be given to every line. Intention had to be found, yet without that over-striving for meanings that never existed. For Mr. Leigh, Edith Evans made his production of As You Like It; he did not have to contribute much except a decent cast, staging, lighting; interpretation was not as unified as that of Esme Church, the director of the 1937 production. Miss Church emphasized a unified effort between cast, technical crew and director. The result was that Miss Evans' Rosalind was complimented by costumes and scenery which seemed in accord with her modish elegance. The performance by Miss Evans glittered and dazzled audiences because it was a total conception – a Watteau style Arden with a fascinating Rosalind.

Technically, the 1926 production did not compare to the 1937 production. Mr. Leigh's choice of costumes was made randomly and by what was most convenient for the Theatre. He did not bother to conceive of a total production. Miss Evans was his focus, but her strength as Rosalind controlled his interpretation of As You Like It. In the 1937 production, Molly McArthur created black and white costumes in eighteenth century style. As Ganymede, Miss Evans wore black knee breeches, and as Rosalind a lacy gown. Her costumes enhanced the performance, but did not detract. The scenery was elaborate, with flowers and fountains, but did not disturb the action. The beauty of Molly McArthur's designs complimented the talented and vivacious Edith Evans.

Clearly, Edith Evans played Rosalind with technical control and inspired acting. She demonstrated her ability to find the sub-conscious of the character, give in to that discovery, and freely played each intention. She showed her mastery of comic timing. Most importantly, Miss Evans played each performance as though it were her last. Her love for acting and her devotion to her craft lead her to cherish being Rosalind; her directors could feel this and her audience could sense this. Her transformation was complete. She was truly Rosalind.

Katharine Hepburn

Miss Hepburn's portrayal of Rosalind was unostentatious and whole-hearted although she lacked the tenderness, sweetness, truthfulness and lovely voice of Edith Evans. Her characterization of Rosalind was merely an impersonation of her idea of the character rather than a transformation into her. To compensate for his flaw in her performance, Miss Hepburn spoke each line with extreme care, played in a straightforward manner, and relied on "her grace, breeding, and matter-of-fact elegance" (Brown 239) which gave her a very special glamour. Lovely to look at as she gracefully moved across the stage, Miss Hepburn seemed to be aware of her own physical beauty complimented by her chiseled cheekbones. She spoke each line clearly and with fortitude, but did not support her verbal message with facial expressions. She moved through Mr. Bailey's scenery inspiring audiences to praise her as Katharine Hepburn who was performing in <u>As You Like It</u>, not as Rosalind. The actress only illustrated an idea of Rosalind; she did not become Rosalind. Her portrayal was not an honest presentation of her conception of her comic heroine; but Katharine Hepburn only used one dimension of Rosalind, her romanticism. She did not attempt to create Rosalind's human side or her witty comic edge. The actress remained on one level in her performance, in idealized romantic tomboy.

Miss Hepburn over prepared herself to play the role. She studied vocally every day for six months before the opening, and involved herself with every aspect of the production. In a personal interview with Katharine Hepburn one week before opening performance of the production in Cleveland, William F. McDermott questioned her about her approach to the role (McDermott 1950, Sect. 2, p.1, Col. 3). She revealed her interpretation of Rosalind in her answers. She said:

> <u>As You Like It</u> *is all dreaming and hoping, wonder and magic. It reminds me of when I first went to New York to try my fortune. I was so happy and so wild with excitement that my feet never touched the pavement....I am getting some of the same kind of pleasure out of trying* <u>As You Like It</u>. *The Kids like this play....We play it for romance – pure, idealized, fabulous romance.*
>
> *I studied for six months three hours a day under the tutelage of Constance Collier...and developed more breath, range and color of voice.*
>
> *I don't want to be bumptious (As Rosalind)....There is no thigh-slapping no athletics, no leaping.*

These comments summarize her visions of Rosalind: a one-sided romantic one. The actress posed, smiled abundantly, and played the happy romantic. Mr. McDermott concluded his article by pointing out that Miss Hepburn impressed him as "a modest, courageous and gallant young woman who was approaching her Broadway trial with some hope and great trepidation" (McDermott). Criticism of her acting reveals this. She did not recreate the inner spirit of Rosalind. She created a fairy-tale image of her.

The director of the production, Michael Benthall, did not stage the production with the idea of complimenting Miss Hepburn. He conceived of <u>As You Like It</u> as a mood piece and relied just as much on his technical crew as he did on his cast. His staging was designed with individuality and imagination, but the cast appeared to be too directed to relax in their roles. "Under Mr. Benthall's heavy-accented direction, the performance was singularly busy" (Atkinson); everyone moved around the amorous forest with such pretty skipping and traipsing that the performance lacked emotional depth. His direction of the first wooing scene focused on creating interesting pictures through poses and gestures, but Miss Hepburn and Mr. Prince played on a one-dimensional level. The actress spoke each line with clarity but did not add inner feeling. Mr. Prince was a handsome partner, but did not seem overwhelmingly in love. The result of his direction was a scene played to show how Rosalind loved Orlando and nothing more. Mr. Benthall was concerned with an overall conception of <u>As You Like It</u> which would create the ideal environment of <u>As You Like It</u> which would create the ideal environment for love. Sadly, he emphasized the large conception without developing the characters to their fullest potential. The production was an over-produced and under-acted romantic frolic which appealed to the eye. He reduced the play to two lovely and laggard acts (Barnes), and tried to fill it with bird's songs, owl hoots, a snowstorm, garlanded processionals, wood smoke, choruses, and a fine chamber orchestra.

Technically, the production was sumptuous. James Bailey's gorgeous scenery and costumes demanded most of the attention of the audience. Reviewers all agree that the final scene with the marriage festivities was designed with keen imagination and technical beauty. However, the technical prowess of this production outshined the acting quality. The audience never stopped focusing on the music, costumes, or scenery for they provided the excitement inherent in the production. The performers merely added to the technical beauty.

Katharine Hepburn's one-sided portrayal was a result of her own personal interpretation of the role, Mr. Benthall's strict direction and Mr. Bailey's dominant scenery and costumes. These factors deterred her from developing into a more truthful Rosalind. The major problem with this production of <u>As You Like It</u> seemed to be the fault of the producers representing the Theatre Guild. Theresa Helburn and Lawrence Langner, production supervisors, were interested in the audience attraction of Miss Hepburn. They exploited her career to promote their organization. They shipped Mr. Benthall from England to make an impression on American audiences that the Theatre Guild's presentation of <u>As You Like It</u> would be a quality production because they employed a British director. So the flaw with this production was that it was produced to bring the Theatre Guild commercial success. The director, actress and crew did not work together as one unit. Although Miss Hepburn involved herself in every aspect of the production, her assistance was not sufficient to unify the efforts of the cast and crew.

Vanessa Redgrave

Vanessa Redgrave's interpretation of Rosalind incorporated all the complexities inherent in the character. As age twenty-four, Miss Redgrave utilized the Stanislavsky System as her guide and played for action and emotion. Her only setback in her portrayal of Rosalind was her obvious self-consciousness about her acting technique. She displayed a quivering lip and make awkward gestures at times. Despite these moments when she revealed her inexperience in playing Shakespeare, "she fully possessed Rosalind's special quality — that of investing what is most serious to her with the charm of an exquisite frolic" (London Times, 11 January 1962). In her sudden involuntary tenderness she was quite unaffected and most touching. Her performance glowed from within and illuminated the rest of the stage. In her portrayal, she departed completely from the romanticism which Katharine Hepburn relied on, and she played the scenes in which Rosalind is in disguise with comic brilliance. "The richness of her comedy depended on the constant uncertainty of whether the woman in love would be able to keep up the masquerade" (Wardle).

In the first wooing scene (III. ii.) Vanessa Redgrave relaxed into her characterization of Rosalind and began to enjoy her acting. She played the scene with freedom of movement, lying on the floor, and emphasizing the fun of playing a boy. Her youth was an asset in this scene; she not only played the frolic and delight which Rosalind feels but she instilled the spirit of youth and the passion for love. The only flaw in her interpretation was that she seemed too girlishly ecstatic at times. For a few brief moments she showed inexperience.

Vanessa Redgrave's conception and portrayal of Rosalind were the outcome of her close relationship with the director, Michael Elliott. He was the most outstanding director of all four in question. He designed the production, paying close attention to all facets, especially the acting quality. Vanessa Redgrave's performance was so well defined and complex because of his meticulous work to make it that way. This production was a product of his genius. Vanessa Redgrave relied on his conception of the play. Mr. Elliott interpreted the journey through the Forest of Arden as the place where every character except Jaques found himself and the place they love (Goodman). He believed that As You Like It was a comic romance which presented the ambiguity of Elizabethan romance. In his staging, Mr. Elliott sought to define the movement of the play from darkness or chaos to light or comic resolution. He collaborated with his light technician, Mr. Richard Pilbrow, to create mood lighting. His production emphasized the complexities of the pastoral world. To do so, he took advantage of director's license and staged the stalking and killing of a deer to suggest a reason for Jaques melancholy (Lambert). Michael Elliott's approach was an attempt to give the play cohesion and a sense of movement. In the final scene, he treated the wedding ceremonies very seriously. Romantic frivolity was undercut by a solemn tone which was intimate and sincere.

Richard Negri provided simply designed scenery and costumes. A massive oak standing on a green mound proved to be the perfect set piece around which the performers moved. Mr. Negri's technical expertise allowed him to create set and costume designs which added to the life of the production but did not detract from it. Thus, Elliott was free to concentrate on the characters and incidents on which the buoyancy of the comedy depends and to get from the company a livelier and well-balanced performance.

Thus Vanessa Redgrave's Rosalind was complimented by the technical aspects of the production. Her interpretation stemmed from her close relationship with and total trust in Michael Elliott. Although her characterization was awkward at times, she played with a strong supporting cast against a simple setting which aided her interpretation. This production was a unified effort and its success depended on the talent of the cast, the director, and the technical crew.

They have their exits and their entrances;

Chapter Three

Four conclusions concerning methods of producing <u>As You Like It</u> and interpretations of Rosalind in the twentieth century emerge from this study: (1) methods of theatrical production changed between 1926 and 1961 as illustrated by the comparison of four productions of <u>As You Like It</u>; (2) Esme Church directed the most outstanding production of <u>As You Like It</u>; (3) though Edith Evans, Katharine Hepburn and Vanessa Redgrave approached the role with similar acting techniques, they interpreted Rosalind differently; (4) Edith Evans gave the most successful performance of Rosalind.

To determine the quality of each production, I have focused on three requirements which are necessary for the director to achieve: the director should (1) create the elements of pastoral comedy; (2) inspire and prepare the performances to play the characters with skillful comic timing and believable characterizations; and (3) unify the production into a company effort with the cast and crews working together in rehearsals and performances. The only director in question to meet all of the requirements was Esme Church who directed Edith Evans in 1937. Because Andrew Leigh, Michael Benthall and Michael Elliott were weak in one of these criteria for success, their productions did not achieve the audience reception, outstanding reviews or success of the 1937 production of <u>As You Like It.</u>

In 1926, Andrew Leigh directed <u>As You Like It</u> as one of a series of productions for a season at the Old Vic. His directorial process derived from those directors which came before him, so he did not use his own imagination in his conception of <u>As You Like It.</u> Instead of analyzing the play and developing his own interpretation of it, he followed what had been done in previous productions at the Old Vic and in England. He cut long speeches, relied on his leading lady, Edith Evans, to perform Rosalind so well that the production would be successful, and used old costumes and sets from the storerooms of the Old Vic. As a result of his lack of imagination in direction, he did not create a unified production. In fact, though he prepared the other performers adequately, he focused on Edith Evans as the performer who would inspire his audience. Andrew Leigh created the elements of pastoral comedy only. He showed the world of Arden and its joys and sorrows thanks to the genius and inspired performance of one actress: Edith Evans.

Esme Church created a production of <u>As You Like It</u> in 1937 which featured the elements of pastoral comedy, offered excellent performances by all members of the cast, and appeared as a unified effort between the cast and crews. She directed the play with more imagination than Mr. Leigh and instilled into her direction her own interpretation of Arden and its inhabitants. Miss Church did not cut the original text. She based her directorial process on the necessity for each performer to excel. In particular, she developed the relationship between Rosalind (Edith Evans) and Orlando (Michael Redgrave). Her understanding of Shakespeare's intention in <u>As You Like It</u> was clear in her direction; she believed Arden as a pastoral world free from the cares of the court but filled with its own juxtaposition of the fantasy world and the real world and used Rosalind's satirical wit to point out the pitfalls of love. At the same time, she showed how important romantic love is to the play, and worked with Molly McArthur in her creation of lovely scenery and costumes to depict a warm romantic Arden. She used visual effects to add to the performer; she did not show a fantasy world of frivolous characters. She inspired characterizations which were believable and skillfully executed. Furthermore, her direction resulted in a unified production with each cast member offering good performance that supported her interpretation of the world of Arden.

Michael Benthall's production of <u>As You Like It</u> epitomized the problems of producing Shakespeare. The production, commercially successful because it featured the popular film star, Katharine Hepburn, was full of lavishly designed scenery, costumes, lighting, and music. Although the production was visually exciting, it was not an honest performance. Mr. Benthall's interpretation had only one point; Arden is full of romantic love. He did not attempt to illustrate the paradoxes of the pastoral world as Esme Church did. He relied on a one-sided version of Arden. Mr. Benthall cut the play to two acts. He filled the production with busy movements but did not inspire quality performances from every performer. He based the production on Miss Hepburn's audience appeal and exploited her physical beauty. He seemed more interested in posing her during her speeches to show off her legs than in her characterization. It is ironic that this production had audience appeal and so little acting quality. Perhaps, if it had been performed in England an audience more familiar with Shakespeare would have recognized the flaws of the production. Mr. Benthall did not seem interested in a unified production effort, but in a commercially successful version of <u>As You Like It</u> to boost the career of Hepburn.

Michael Elliott presented a unified production of <u>As You Like It</u> in 1961 fulfilling all the necessary requirements of producing Shakespeare. However, in comparison to Esme Church's, Mr. Elliott's conception seems too modern. He used extremely simple set and costumes in the hopes of basing his production on the quality of the acting. The production was uneven because of this: some performers were better than others and some scenes were played with more skill and believability than others. Mr. Elliott is a fine director who created the elements of pastoral comedy, inspired and prepared the performers, and unified the production. He developed a rationale for every action and event in the play, and trained his cast to perform freely. The stage set became Arden because each character believed it was that place. Mr. Elliott did not require fancy scenery and lavish costumes to create the forest. The production's flaw was the inexperience of some of his cast to execute his interpretation. Vanessa Redgrave, only twenty-four, played a youthful witty Rosalind but did not seem in control of the character at all times.

Mr. Elliott's method of producing Shakespeare in 1961 is different from Andrew Leigh's method in 1926. The twentieth century director grew in his ability to create an imaginative interpretation of Shakespeare's As You Like It. Andrew Leigh was a product of the past; he produced Shakespeare according to the practices of the eighteenth and nineteenth centuries. Esme Church and Michael Elliott used the modern approach to Shakespeare. They used the full script and created unified productions based on their particular visions. Michael Benthall succumbed to the commercialism of the film industry of our modern era. His method was based on audience appeal instead of quality acting. In conclusion, the methods of producing Shakespeare in the twentieth century are defined through the four productions in this study. The change in directorial process allowed the director more control over the total production, and to the extent to which he was able to unify all aspects of the production according to his own individual interpretation, he was successful. The method of direction which each used directly affected the performances.

Edith Evans, Katharine Hepburn, and Vanessa Redgrave approach acting in the same manner. They carefully study the play, analyze the role, and prepare both mind and body to transform into the character. Evans believed that acting was fun and should be done naturally. She prepared to play Rosalind by first understanding the meaning of every word. She worked very closely with her director to understand his expectations and interpretations. Practicing on her own was important to Miss Evans. Understanding the scene by herself was imperative to playing it with the other character. Katharine Hepburn also believed in preparing months ahead for a production. Her study for Rosalind required six months of arduous practice to correct her New England accent and to learn how to speak clearly. She studied the period and before she entered the rehearsal period was knowledgeable about Elizabethan England. She enjoyed the study process just as much as performing. Similarly, Vanessa Redgrave relied on preparation for the role as the foundation for her portrayal of Rosalind. She carefully analyzed each line and intention, constantly working to interpret the role as her director dictated. She understood the point of the play and tried to act all sides of the character. For Miss Redgrave, the acting process is based on a clear conception of the purpose of the play. In fact, all three Shakespearean heroines believed in preparation as the most important process in playing Rosalind.

Although the approach of each actress to the role of Rosalind was similar, their interpretations were quite different. Edith portrayed Rosalind as a satirical yet tender woman who controlled the inhabitants of Arden; Katharine emphasized Rosalind's romantic qualities and little more, and Vanessa played a youthful Rosalind captivated by her desire for love but witty and playful as well. Edith Evans was the actress who transformed into the character with the most technical control and truthful acting. She played the character with the vivacity, good humor, gentleness and technical skill to be the Rosalind who captivates and entertains.

Edith Evans played Rosalind in 1926 and 1937 under different directors but with the same skill and enthusiasm. She presented a mature view of the heroine, revealing the many sides of the character. Her portrayal was relaxed and natural. She did not seem to work at Rosalind; she was Rosalind. Edith Evans gave the most successful performance because she was in total control throughout each performance. When she was on stage she demanded the audience's attention. Her portrayal seemed to illuminate the stage. Miss Evans demanded the respect of the audience. Her fine acting technique and her ability to become the character enabled her to play Rosalind as Shakespeare must have intended.

Katharine Hepburn portrayed the heroine as she portrayed every other character she played on stage or in films. She was herself on stage. Hepburn did not transform into Rosalind Miss Evans did. Instead, she played her as a romantic woman who smiled and posed. The actress demanded the audience's attention because of her previous stage and film successes, and was praised as "Hepburn in Arden." Her performance was one dimensional. She was so concerned with speaking clearly that she performed, but did not allow herself to live the emotions of Rosalind. She played a beautiful woman who was hopelessly in love.

Vanessa Redgrave did not have enough experience to achieve the perfection of Edith, but she was excellent in her portrayal of Rosalind as a youthful, witty girl. Her performance lacked only the maturity and technical control of Edith. Miss Redgrave should be praised for her depiction of Rosalind's humor and wit. The actress was in total control when she was disguised as Ganymede. She illustrated the fun in impersonation and yet seemed to have the instinctive fear of being caught in her disguise at any moment. Miss Redgrave's flaws were in her transition from Ganymede to Rosalind; she did not depict Rosalind's tenderness as well as Evans did. Vanessa also encountered problems because of her height. She made awkward gestures and seemed to work too hard at trying to relax; she created the second best performance of Rosalind in the twentieth century.

As a result of this investigative study, I have found that the role of Rosalind demands much from the actress. Rosalind has more sides and more puns than any other of Shakespeare's women. The role gives the actress a chance to achieve a modulation between the brassiness needed to enjoy being in disguise and the tenderness needed to portray love. Evans gave the most successful performance to Rosalind in the twentieth century. She discovered moments of sweetness that stage historians praise as moments which will never be forgotten. She transformed into Rosalind and portrayed her as the delightful comic heroine who captivates and entertains in the Forest of Arden.

CHAPTER FOUR

KATHARINE HEPBURN

Her real name was Katharine Houghton Hepburn. Her birthday was December 5, 1907 and birthplace was Hartford, Connecticut, USA.

Katharine Hepburn relished playing independent women (winning four Academy Awards during her amazing career) and made no excuses for her high-profile love affairs, individualistic fashion and obvious strength. She was named Best Classic Actress of the 20th Century in an Entertainment Weekly on-line poll on September 1999; Ranked #1 woman in the AFI's '50 greatest movie legends' on June 1999; Ranked #68 in Empire (UK) magazine's "The Top 100 Movie Stars of All Time" list in October 1997.

I traveled to New York City to revisit Broadway and see a current production of Wicked. I had the pleasure to viewing the last performance of Idina Menzel as Elphaba. In the foyer of the Gershwin Theatre where I viewed the production, a portrait of Katharine Hepburn appears. Her brilliant portrayal brought the remembrances that carry us to developing the legacy of Hepburn, our memories of her, our hopes for books and films about her and most importantly, a renewal of fine art as a way of life, education, and living.

My work spans forty years of study of Katharine Hepburn as I have watched her as a star in her life and as a legacy in her death. In fact, I have initiated a stage history revolution in my work as a writer and artist for the past thirty years. When my thesis project seemed to be impossible to approve because of lack of research I sought the help of Katharine Hepburn who suggested the Lincoln Center Reference Library for the Performing Arts. The committee of Lehigh University English Department under the direction of Professor Frank Hook passed my proposal when I suggested that I go to the cultural center of New York City to do the research. From that day forward, I have always sought the help of the reference library at Lincoln Center and pursuit of my dream to be a stage historian. With this work, I initiate my publishing career in the field to pay tribute to those who have gone before me to teach about fine art as a way of life and a way of study for students of all ages.

In a personal letter which I received from Katharine Hepburn dated February 26, 1980, she answered my request for information concerning her performance as follows:

Dear Mary Ann Pasda,

I am sorry but I really do not have the time to answer sensibly that list of questions and I have no records of anything. Try the Lincoln Center Library.

At the time of the writing of the letter, Miss Hepburn lived in West Hartford, Connecticut.

The preeminent philosophy of the fine artist is development of the inner soul to portray characters and the goal extends to an entire life of devotion to fine art. Therefore, the soul is preoccupied with spiritual dimensions of soul rather than temporal activities.

This is why fine art as a formative creative force in education would save our children.

The fine art legacy of Hepburn points a way to educate our children with care and compassion rather than the current system. Hepburn's life is a microcosm that will establish the thesis of this work: build a curriculum for students from pre-school to adulthood based on the right side of the brain to enhance the left side and to allow the duality of brain function to supersede the academic goals so that the student CAN LEARN. If we focus on Hepburn as an example of a new way of life for us all, we learn that we can become more talented and more joyous than we are now. The reason? Fine art enhances the human spirit and enriches our lives to allow us to be who we really are.

The basic review of the works on Hepburn that are most current show us that her life was one of joyous self pursuit while she cared for family and friends as well.

Anne Edwards in <u>Katharine Hepburn A Remarkable Woman</u> offers a great basic biography with theatrical as well as film and television history. The work is very detailed and superior in biographical form. Her bibliography is useful for scholars to enhance papers and works about the actress. Next, a recent work entitled <u>Kate Remembered</u> by A. Scott Berg acts as the official final chronicle of her final years. My work in its present state adds to these works and pursues a different course: Kate as legacy for educational revolution.

The demands and enthusiasm that the acting career require and the means and methods that women in the arts use to pursue careers can be documented and studied as a part of our recording history so vital in fine arts. Interestingly, Edith Evans and Vanessa Redgrave provide a starting point for this study to show how other women have succeeded in the twentieth century. Our vision of our own Katharine Hepburn and her ability to be a great woman and actress are the focus of this new chapter.

Katharine Hepburn, as a young woman, became an instant success on the American stage and in motion pictures. She was a spirited performer unafraid of challenges and commonly took political stands and accepted roles that tested her acting ability. She introduced into film a strength of character previously considered undesirable in Hollywood leading ladies. A role model for women throughout the world, she is noted for her brisk New England accent, unique rare beauty, wit and independence. She will remain one of the most beloved actresses in the archives of American history.

Essentially a reference work in nature, <u>The Legacy of Katharine Hepburn</u>, theoretically seeks to place lists of references works available during the time of printing into the view of readers so they can write, read, and learn about the life and many works of Hepburn as well as the importance of those works in a fine arts context. Therefore, I refer to the life time of Katharine Hepburn as a zenith in the cultural area of achievement for women in the fine arts. Her formidable life presents a way to be present in the arts as a leader and a true heroine in the real sense of the word. The nature of art lends itself to this type of reference work as students especially need to realize the depth of commitment that a career in the fine arts requires. I have added this chapter to my updated thesis and created a book to deepen the understanding of youth as well as those who seek to know Hepburn as a fine artist and a creator of characters as well as a very remarkable lifetime during the twentieth-century. If we study how she lived we can learn how to educate our children and how to create a better world since her spirit is one of peace and individuality. She loved her work, her family, and herself.

My semi-biographical chapter focuses on Katharine Hepburn as fine artist who surpassed others in her devotion to the craft of theatre art. As my mother met Hepburn, but I never did, I have only recollections from my own life as a predecessor of Kate and a follower of her devotion to fine art as a way of life. I seek to enthrall the reader with details from her past that have come to me from my own life watching her films, listening to her few interviews, and reading books about her. Her private life was just that and I respect her wishes to remain a true legacy and icon in the midst of a daily life that she often worked very hard to keep secret. I write according to the current trend of data that has recently been created about Kate. Legacy after all is the past left to us to have forever. We have her tenacity to drama as a cornerstone of a lifetime of commitment to the beauty of life. Even in her decisions to write biographical material with editors and others, she was purposeful. In my study for this current work, I came across A. Scott Berg's work entitled Kate Remembered, a delightful work that tells of Berg's twenty year friendship with Hepburn and his views of Kate's later years as paramount to remembering her. I also recall Katharine Hepburn's own work Me which is a collection of thoughts on activities in life which is now a famous work. Even the notes from this work have been auctioned off as memorabilia of the late great actress. My work complements these best books and offers the reader a way to carry on Kate's way of life as an artist.

During the era in which she lived, Katharine was often interpreted as eccentric in her independent character. Interestingly, collections that list famous Kate quotations use the word to describe her! But in our new cultural awakening, Katharine Hepburn offers a feminist spirit to women and a universal love of life to all humans. My chapter on Hepburn is unique. Those of us who loved Kate for her independence and tenacity often dream of her as still alive. Alas, I do often dream of her as a mentor to me in my own creative mind. I feel this is a positive note for all creative artists and for educators who wish to reinvent education to bring new life to our society.

Katharine Hepburn was a tenacious actress who lived a life according to the mandate of fine art as a way of life. Her decision in college to pursue the study of drama and act was pivotal to her career. She never stopped living a life based on platonic creative idealism and her talent showed in her ability to play characters especially on film. Kate's educational experiences dictated the life she would lead. Ultimately, the artist must have something to say for mastery over form is not the goal as much as adapting form to inner meaning.

We must survive as a species based on our functioning educational views to raise human beings who can act in accordance with principles. These are clearly a part of the fine arts. Photographers see more that the regular eye and show children and adults how to make pictures of moments to cherish. Dancing is the most comprehensive and beautiful of the arts as we move our bodies in the flow of time and space. I started as a ballet dancer and find that I still move today through the arts of yoga and t'ai chi.

Theatre teaches us to be lively people. In fact, Shakespeare's chief effort is always to make good drama with contrast and conflict with modification of characters from historical records. Art teaches us to portray our inner selves through color and music seems to uphold our spiritual centers. I outline these qualifications in my work throughout as I explore ways to intertwine the study of fine arts in day to day educational systems.

We can learn from Katharine Hepburn and use her life as a paradigm for this new educational system. Chapter Four weaves anecdotes, fact, history, and biographical data into a macrocosm for the reader to create a blue print for their own life success. The Socratic method lends itself to the legacy of Hepburn and provides a starting point for children to be influenced and motivated by the freedoms that the fine arts in education offer. Know thyself as a maxim of the method suggests that children are taught to be independent learners right from the beginning and are allowed to think independently in the open classroom where the art spirit will have something to say and master its own destiny. For example, in the art classes I teach, I seek to find ways to teach each child on an individual basis and adapt my class to that child's needs.

In 1950, a young woman traveled on a bus with friends to New York City to see the play <u>As You Like It</u> by William Shakespeare at the Cort Theatre. It was a brisk fall night when the women entered the theatre to witness a delightful Katharine Hepburn play Rosalind. After the show, the four women walked backstage unassumingly to see if they might catch a glimpse of Hepburn, the young well known actress who was twenty years their senior and who they admired for her independent spirit and witty nature both on and off stage. According to the account by my mother, one of the women, Hepburn greeted them in a hallway with a gracious tone to her manner. Entirely at ease with her fans, Hepburn loved to chat and shake hands. It was this evening that promoted me to write my original thesis and this book about Hepburn. Her gracious attitude toward fans and her love of theatre helped create the magic that held audiences captive in the twentieth and I predict for many centuries in the future. She was a woman who respected the fact that people came to see her perform and that also respected her privacy. She only granted five television interviews in her entire career and did some radio in the 30's and 40's.

Legacy: a strong word which implies that we learn from the past of Katharine Hepburn. The reader might ask why I select to call my work a legacy. I have become the fine artist and writer that I am today due to the influences of the great actress Katharine Hepburn; I have studied her life and work and present my answers about why her legacy is important. Her voice was a true liberation one that resounded throughout the entire century. Based on fine arts training commencing with initiation into ballet guilds, theatrical groups, and musical recitals, I learned to perform Chopin Concertos, Shakespearean Soliloquies, and paint landscapes by the age of nine. The following work announces to the entire globe that children should be educated in the fine arts before, during and after training in reading, writing, and mathematics. The brain will be prepared for learning by preparation that will allow personal growth through fine art. This paradigm is based on my life and work which has relied heavily on the legacy of Katharine Hepburn.

I have selected to focus on the career or Katharine Hepburn for this chapter as related to my own life. Her legacy is my legacy. She has been my guide as I work through my life filled with career and the promise of creating my own legacy as a writer and artist.

Moreover, I have relied on conversation and interviews with my mother, J.D. Pasda, who also lived Hepburn's acting and performing gift and often used quotations from Hepburn to teach life's lessons.

As I update my work to design a twenty-first century quest for a way to reflect on Hepburn's career as a cornerstone for women in the age of technology and argue that the most exceptional function of stage history in our new age should be as a viable academic subject and major available to students in academic settings. I first look back on the day she died and my personal journals where I kept notes on Hepburn's career. CNN carried the following few words that changed my life forever. "Screen and stage legend Katharine Hepburn died Sunday afternoon at her home in Old Saybrook, Connecticut. She was 96." Quickly, I wrote down the words and noted that I might reinvent my thesis and tell the world how she helped me identify myself as a woman.

Hepburn's bold, distinctive personality delighted me as a child. She inherited from her doctor father and suffragette mother her three most pronounced traits: an open and ever-expanding mind, a healthy body (maintained through constant rigorous exercise), and an inability to tell anything less than the truth. Furthermore, a message of hope lies within the depth of performances by Hepburn. In my current study, I have watched all her films again to recall the special significance of each in time and in relationship to my premise that her performances held the secrets of feminism. This chapter holds my answers, efforts to solve the questions that lie within all feminine beings to create personal life answers. My answers were part of the legacy of Hepburn and in fact, are based on her life. So, in this chapter that is the new addition to my study from 1979-1980, I present the findings in order of decades applicable to my life based on the career of Hepburn, an actual true legacy. These courageous women pave a new way for us to seek personal fulfillment.

Hepburn acts in death as a stronger and formidable woman that she was in life. First of all, her roles span a century and present truths about the female psyche that are evident in the characterizations and preparation by Hepburn.

Next, Hepburn consumed an entire century of audiences who lived her work. Her ability to be Hepburn is noteworthy and offers a pattern of a life time for career women. Lastly, Hepburn dignifies the status of women in the theater film industry as well as the passion area. She lived in faith developed by and dependent on her craft of acting and worked with hope to give a fine example for how to live. As artists, we seek to repay the talents we have, create deeds that provoke a spiritual atmosphere around us and continue to produce creative endeavors that produce the creative spiritual in our lifetime. Hepburn was aware of her influence and conjured a life that spiritually filled her psyche with dimensions to produce a legacy.

Adaptive to cultural and social as well as historical challenges, Hepburn changes her own personality to fit her roles and in so doing offers women visions of their own abilities to change themselves within different decades. Her career spans a century. Characters offer moral statements as well as cultural segmentations that present truths about women's roles. Messages of hope are within the roles. The history of the characters performed by Hepburn suggest behaviors, moral and decisiveness toward a new vision of women.

The first decade of her life was her birth on May 12th, 1907; the second decade found her education; the third decade began her career with her first and subsequent New York productions; the fourth decade lead to her screen career; the fifth decade continued with screen and stage roles; the sixth and seventh decades develop stage and screen roles; the eight decade found the actress in television movies; the ninth decade found her last film appearance and the tenth decade was her last. In listing aspects of my own life biographical data intertwined with the Hepburn filmography, I allow the reader to see how the actress influenced my life choices and encouraged me by example to be myself in all my endeavors.

Twentieth Century: First Decade

Aristotle defined art as imitation. I offer the reader the opportunity to imitate the life of Katharine Hepburn in the manner of trying to make every decade on this earth momentous in activity with personal choices for career and family that fulfill and rely on fine art as a basis for life itself. Fine arts offer a power that improves and directs the human spirit to be a servant of a nobler purpose: to search deeply into the soul, develop and tend it, to make art the shell that covers the human potential.

The following theatre television film lists were taken from my original thesis notes my journals or my mother's reflections and span eight centuries of performances by Hepburn. I note theatre, television, or film next to the entry. The brief commentary offers summation of biography and application to my premise that Kate offers a legacy that I have applied to my own life.

Second Decade: 20's

Summer Stock Theatre (1928)

The Big Pond (1928)

The Czarina (1928)

The Cradle Snatchers (1928)

New York Theatre (1928-29)

These Days (1928)

Holiday (1928)

Death Takes a Holiday (1929)

Kate's age of conscious creation began in college. The composition of a life parallels the fortitude of the artist in motion when they try to find a career path. So, instrumental to Kate' life legacy is the moment when she started to act. At Bryn Mawr, she became active in theatrical productions, and after her senior year she appeared in two productions in Baltimore. That same year, she moved to New York to begin training as an actor, and appeared in her first New York production, *The Big Pond*.

We follow Hepburn in our journey to become a separate entity from our loved ones, although we live very deeply.

Third Decade: 30's

New York Theatre (1930)

A Month in the Country (1930)

Summer Stock (1930)

The Admirable Crichton (1930)

The Romantic Young Lady) (1930)

Romeo and Juliet (1930)Art and Mrs. Bottle (1930)

Summer Stock (1931)

The Animal Kingdom (1931)

The Warrior's Husband (1931)

Summer Stock (1932)

The Bride The Sun Shines On (1932)

The Lake (1933)

Jane Eyre (1936)

The Philadelphia Story (1939)

Films

Holiday (1938)

Bringing Up Baby (1938)

Stage Door (1937)

Quality Street (1937)

Woman Rebels, A (1936)

Mary of Scotland (1936)

Sylvia Scarlett (1936)

Alice Adams (1935) Katharine Hepburn Nominated for Academy
  Award

Break of Hearts (1935)

Little Minister, The (1934)

Spitfire (1934)

Little Women (1933)

Morning Glory (1933) Katharine Hepburn won Academy Award
for Best Actress

Christopher Strong (1933)

Bill of Divorcement, A (1932)

Thematic unity incredibly follows as we study the plot and
circumstance of her first major Academy Award for Best Actress. The
film seems to mirror the life of the actress. Morning Glory (1933) is
the story of a naive and pretentious aspiring actress, starring Katharine
Hepburn in only her third film. This RKO film, directed by Lowell
Sherman and adapted from a stage play by Zoe Akins, is notable since
it helped to launch the actress' successful career, and provided her with
the first (of four) Best Actress Oscars - the film's only nomination. Many
critics have noted that Hepburn should have won an Oscar for her
first screen appearance in *A Bill of Divorcement (1932)* a year earlier.
(Katharine Hepburn) is an inexperienced, mall town community theatre
actress from a New England (Vermont) country town who comes to
New York stagestruck, bringing with her a letter from George Bernard
Shaw, and ambitious dreams of becoming a Broadway theatrical star.
She states: "I have something very wonderful in me, you'll see."

She makes new friends quickly including kindly veteran stage actor
Robert Harley Hedges (C. Aubrey Smith), who befriends her. When
she first meets him, she explains her name: I hope you're going to tell
me your name. I want you for my first friend in New York. Mine's Eva
Lovelace. It's partly made up and partly real. It was Ada Love. Love's
my family name. I added the 'lace.' Do you like it, or would you prefer
something shorter? A shorter name would be more convenient on a sign.
Still, 'Eva Lovelace in *Camille*,' for instance, or 'Eva Lovelace in *Romeo
and Juliet*' sounds very distinguished, doesn't it? At a cocktail party
held by a successful but troubled and temperamental star Rita Vernon
(Mary Duncan,) Eva becomes drunk on champagne, and performs two

Shakespearean soliloquies for the party guests with slurred speech. She stuns the guests with her portrayal of the balcony scene from *Romeo and Juliet*. Ambitious young playwright Joseph Sheridan (Douglas Fairbanks, Jr.) arranges for her to be the understudy for Rita in a new show that he has written. On opening night, Rita demands more money from the slimy producer Louis Easton (Adolphe Menjou) just before the curtain goes up, but Easton resists and fires her. Eva takes Rita's place, performing brilliantly.

Backstage following her triumphant performance, she is warned about instant success going to her head by Hedges, like a "morning glory" which blooms beautifully, but then quickly withers and dies. Every year, in every theater, some young person makes a hit.

Sometimes it's a big hit, sometimes a little one. It's a distinct success, but how many of them keep their heads? How many of them work? Youth comes to the fore. Youth has its hour of glory. But too often it's only a morning glory - a flower that fades before the sun is very high. Embracing her maid (Theresa Harria), who at one time was a 'morning glory' star, Eva declares to everyone that she doesn't care if she *is* a morning glory, speaking defiantly: Nellie, they've all been trying to frighten me. They've been trying to frighten me into being sensible, but they can't do it. Not now. Not yet. They've got to let me be as foolish as I want to be. I-I want to ride through the crowd. I want to- I want to go buy me a mink coat. And I'll buy you a beautiful present. And Mr. Hedges! I'll buy Mr. Hedges a little house. And it'll have rooms full of white orchids. And they've got to tell me that I'm much more wonderful than anyone else because, Nellie - Nellie, I'm not afraid. I'm not afraid of being just a morning glory. I'm not afraid. I'm not afraid. I'm not afraid. Why should I be afraid? I'm not afraid (Dirks).

In my work that solidifies the treatment of goals and dreams as paramount, the legacy of Hepburn and personal achievements is essential to a cultural influences in the fine arts that I experienced at the youthful age of three. I traveled, studied dance, and visited New York City by the age of three. I also suggest that educational theories are founded upon inherent properties of fine arts and that Kate knew this as she pursued her life's work. Many women tell me they just do not have time to study or write or pursue dreams.

Like Hepburn, I also paint for creative enjoyment and have had some notable works in different countries due to commissions. I learned from studying Kate's life and works. I use her films as therapy for continued artistic flow in my daily routine and suggest that my readers rely on Kate's independent spirit in her films to also follow a legacy of creative impulse.

Fourth Decade: 40's

New York Theatre

Without Love (1942)

Films

Adam's Rib (1949)

State of the Union (1948)

Song of Love (1947)

Sea of Grass, The (1947)

Undercurrent (1946)

Without Love (1945)

Dragon Seed (1944)

Keeper of the Flame (1942)

Woman of the Year (1942) Katharine Hepburn Nominated for Academy Award

Philadelphia Story (1940) Katharine Hepburn Nominated for Academy Award

In 1932, Hepburn appeared on Broadway in *The Warrior's Husband*. Her performance was well received, and led to several screen tests, and eventually to a role in the 1932 film *A Bill of Divorcement*. Hepburn received excellent notices for her performance in this film. A string of films followed in the 1930s, including *Morning Glory*, her third film, for which Hepburn received her first Academy Award for Best Actress. In 1933 Hepburn returned to New York to star in the Broadway production of *The Lake*, which turned out to be a critical and commercial failure. Upon her return to Hollywood, she starred in a string of films of varying quality and success, and by 1938 she was labeled "box office poison" by exhibitors who claimed that people weren't paying to see her films. In 1939 Hepburn again returned to New York to star on Broadway, this time in *The Philadelphia Story* as Tracy Lord, a role playwright Philip Barry had written for her. The play was a tremendous success, and Hepburn, who owned the film rights (Howard Hughes had bought them for her), sold them to L.B. Mayer and MGM on the condition that she would star. The movie, like the play, was successful, earning Hepburn, Cary Grant and James Stewart Academy Award nominations (Stewart won).

Hepburn's next film was *Woman of the Year*, her first pairing with Spencer Tracy. Hepburn and Tracy would go on to star together in nine films, and would carry on a love affair for 27 years. With twelve Academy Award nominations and four academy awards, the actress remained popular through the entire century. In a world in which change is a factor we adjust to our environment critically based on our ability to perceive. Again, I rely on my current educational practices in teaching art and writing to explain the fundamental purpose behind the importance of the legacy.

Katharine Hepburn shows us how to adjust by creating something in our lives that is constant and that is representative of ourselves. Children obviously need this to survive and I suggest that even young children are exposed to the humor and joy of Hepburn's films.

Fifth Decade: 50's

New York Theatre

As You Like It (1950)

The Millionairess (1952)

American Shakespeare Festival Stratford Connecticut

The Merchant of Venice (1957)

Much Ado About Nothing (1957)

Suddenly, Last Summer (1959) Katharine Hepburn Nominated for Academy Award

Desk Set, The (1957)

Iron Petticoat, The (1956)

Rainmaker, The (1956) Katharine Hepburn Nominated for Academy Award

Summertime (1955) Katharine Hepburn Nominated for Academy Award

Pat and Mike (1952)

African Queen, The (1951) Katharine Hepburn Nominated for Academy Award

In the 1940s and 50s, Hepburn continued to appear in films and on stage. She received seven Academy Award nominations, and won two Oscars for Best Actress, for Guess Who's Coming to Dinner and The Lion in Winter. On the London stage, she appeared in three Shakespeare plays in 1955, and toured with them in Australia. Hepburn continued on the path of a lifetime career. My birth in 1953 would be a time of success for Hepburn.

I came to know her during our peaceful home evenings when Mom would tell me about Katherine Hepburn when I was just two years old. Women who are exposed to imagination and creative endeavors at an early age tend to be more successful in the pursuit of careers. 1957 she appeared in four more Shakespeare productions in Stratford, CT. Drama is the art which reproduces the human spirit. I suggest that educators apply the aspects of drama in classrooms to broaden the scope of the curriculums and add a statement of purpose to the child's life to reinforce the child's ability to perceive the world and create a learning atmosphere that offers freedom and insight. We see this woman of the century continue in her acting for her life's work with coherence and self determination that inspires and shows directions for an educational system to follow. Plays should be a regular part of the classroom. Children can act out their frustrations and their joys. Playwriting is also an important aspect of the curriculum. I see film as a part of the daily regimen as well. Children can use technology to create hands-on films that show their progress in subjects.

Sixth Decade: 60's

American Shakespeare Festival Stratford Connecticut

Twelfth Night (1960)

Antony and Cleopatra (1960)

Madwoman of Chaillot, The (1969)

Lion in Winter, The (1968) Katharine Hepburn won Academy Award for Best Actress

Guess Who's Coming to Dinner (1967) Katharine Hepburn won Academy Award for Best Supporting Actress

Long Day's Journey into Night (1962) Katharine Hepburn Nominated for Academy Award

New York Theatre   Coco (1969)

In 1960 she appeared in four more Shakespeare productions in Stratford, CT. Her style of acting which portrays herself as the character was a perfect fit for bringing Shakespeare to modern audiences. The greatest shock of the year 1968 was that two actresses in the Best Actress category won the award with an unprecedented <u>exact</u> tie - the *only* one in the Best Actress category in Academy history! [There had been a similar tie in the Best Actor category in 1931/2 between Fredric March (for Dr. Jekyll and Mr. Hyde (1931/2)) and Wallace Beery (for The Champ (1931/2)), but it was a nominal tie. Beery was unofficially one vote short of the vote for March.] The winners to share the Oscar were: twenty-two year-old Barbara Streisand in her film debut (in a role she had perfected on Broadway) as the vaudeville comedienne queen Fanny Brice in Funny Girl, who drifts apart from co-star Omar Sharif due to her success. Streisand shared similar humble origins with the famed Follies star and Katharine Hepburn in her monumental role as the witty, strong-willed, aging Queen Eleanor of Aquitaine in The Lion in Winter, who battles with co-star Peter O'Toole's King Henry II over the succession of Richard I (Anthony Hopkins). Her nomination (her eleventh of twelve career nominations) was a record-breaker in itself - it was the highest number of nominations ever recorded up to that time in the Academy's history. Hepburn's win was also a record for Oscar winners - it was Hepburn's *third* Oscar - she had just won her second Oscar a year earlier - she had won earlier for Morning Glory (1932/3) and Guess Who's Coming to Dinner (1967). No one else had ever accomplished that either.

[Hepburn would win her fourth and final Oscar thirteen years later for **On Golden Pond (1981) (Dirk)**.]

During these years, I was acquainted with Shakespeare through drama instruction; I played minor and major roles in local productions at the early age of twelve. During research years at Pennsylvania State University, I learned that development through drama through work of Jean Piaget and Professor Helen Manful and Manuel Duque would become a primary focus in the academic setting for me. I am convinced that my exposure to drama at such as early age transformed my ability to become myself and pursue my dreams to write about the importance of drama in education.

In 1969 Hepburn took a risk by starring on Broadway in *Coco*, a musical about the life of Coco Chanel. Despite Hepburn's worries about her singing voice, *Coco* had a successful run on Broadway.

Seventh Decade: 70's

New York Theatre

A Matter of Gravity (1976)

Film or Television

Corn is Green, The (1979) television

Oily, Oily, Oxen Free (1978)

Rooster Cogburn (1975)

Love Among the Ruins (1975) television

Delicate Balance, A (1973)

Glass Menagerie, The (1973) television

Trojan Woman, The (1971)

It was during the seventies that Hepburn's neurological illness was more pronounced in her work. I admired her tenacity to work in spite of her ailment and treasure her performances during these years. I also followed the dramatic urge and pursued a degree in Theatre Arts at Pennsylvania State University. Movies were not available on video yet during these years, so I would go the local theatres and watch movies at least once a week. Film was my favorite pastime. My most extraordinary role of the mermaid in a children's play called <u>Ofoti</u> took place these years.

I imagine that my current work may bring a joyous reflection on the life of the actress, Katharine, dear Katharine, and may help us rekindle in our hearts her beautiful life attitude based on the fine arts as a way of life. I remember trying to be just like *Hepburn and act like myself on stage. It worked!*

Below are a few of my accomplishments that were a part of my attempt to follow the legacy of Hepburn:

Creator of Theatre for Seniors at Northampton Community College 1978, Creator of Theatre for Children at the Northampton Community College 1977-78, Pennsylvania Playhouse Actress and Teacher 1967-1977, Northampton Community College - wrote and performed in seven plays with children in my classes, Cape Cod Community College, Penn State University where I performed in <u>Ofoti, Bernarda Alba and St. Joan,</u>

American Theatre Association performance of Opheila in <u>Hamlet,</u> Allentown College of St. Francis DeSales (DeSales University) musicals 1972-73.

Eighth Decade: 80's

New York Theatre

West Side Waltz (1981)

Film or Television

Laura Lansing Slept Here (1988) television

Mrs. Delafield Wants to Marry (1986) television

Grace Quigley (1985)

On Golden Pond (1981) Katharine Hepburn won Academy

Award or Best Actress

I am certain that the legacy of Hepburn controlled my dreams at this segment of my life. I accepted a teaching position and scholarship for graduate work at Lehigh University, a turning point for me. At the same time, I learned that I had a gift for teaching others to write. I held a job as Reading –Writing Lab assistant and helped others write. My love of teaching combined with my love of those who needed help to do what I could do naturally intrigued me to pursue a career in Education of the Fine Arts. I was also offered a position as artist in residence by my mother, a professional artist. I became aware of my love for stage history and voraciously read books on the subject in addition to my regular course work for my Master in English at Lehigh University. I met Professor Frank Hook who was aware that I could act, write plays, and express myself dramatically. In comparison, throughout the 1970s, Hepburn appeared in several television movies, including *Love Among the Ruins* in 1975 with Laurence Olivier, for which she won an Emmy Award. In 1979 she was awarded the Screen Actor's Guild Lifetime Achievement Award. I used this special person as a focus for my academic study and began the idea for this current work.

90's Ninth Decade

One Christmas (1994) television

Love Affair (1994)

This Can't Be Love (1994) television

Man Upstairs, The (1992) television

With my thesis completed, I decided to pursue my own writing school online, writing, and visual art in the 90's and watch the elderly Hepburn in her most marvelous years while I married and raised my only son. Hepburn's record fourth Academy Award for Best Actress was achieved for her work in the 1981 film *On Golden Pond*, co-starring

Henry Fonda. Hepburn's last film work was a brief appearance in the 1994 film *Love Affair*.

Tenth Decade: New Millennium

Katharine Hepburn continued to be active even in her old age, riding her bicycle and swimming in the ocean near her house in Old Saybrook, CT. While she was always somewhat reclusive, she appeared in public less and less as she grew older.

The last few years of her life, with her health declining, she generally remained at home. Katharine Hepburn died in her home, surrounded by loved ones, on June 29, 2003, at the age of 96. Researchers will find countless websites devoted to the actress. In fact, at this time, there are more than 25,000. As I updated my work to design a twenty-first century quest for a way to reflect on Hepburn's career as a cornerstone for women in the age of technology and argue that the most exceptional function of stage history in our new age should be as a viable academic subject.

CHAPTER FIVE

A new stage history of Rosalind still lives and is ongoing. At the time of this writing, Peter Hall directed his daughter in the role of Rosalind at the Kingston Theatre on 24-26 High Street in Kingston upon Thames Surrey KT1 1HL United Kingdom. Rebecca Hall creates the new century's Rosalind in the newest theatrical adventure.

In 2003 at the Swan Theatre (Stratford): Previewed 13 March, Opened 20 March 2003, Closed 8 November 2003, the performance was directed by Gregory Thompson with set designs by Colin Peters, costume designs by Hilary Lewis, lighting by Judith Greenwood and sound by David Stoll Cast: Nina Sosanya as 'Rosalind' with Tim Barlow, Daniel Brocklebank, Branwell Donaghey, Christopher Duncan, David Fielder, Amy Finegan, Naomi Frederick, Bradley Freegard, Patricia Gannon, Natasha Gordon, Michael Hadley, Walter Hall, Martin Hutson, Michael G Jones, John Killoran, Edmund Moriarty, Aaron Neil, Alistair Robins and James Staddon. After initial performances in the Swan, this production will travel to Washington to perform at the Kennedy Center before returning in May for the remainder of the Festival Season in Stratford. Gregory Thompson made his RSC directorial debut with this production. Reviewers bashed this production as unexceptional.

Royal Shakespeare Company of London Associate Director Gregory Doran directed Shakespeare's lyrical and ironic comedy of love as the opening production in the Summer Festival Season 2000. One of this country's leading young classical actors, Alexandra Gilbreath played Shakespeare's witty heroine Rosalind. Critics noted the almost bare white stage, with a more liberating Forest of Arden. Alexandra Gilbreath brought physical energy to Rosalind. Gregory Doran's production always looked good and his inventive designers, Kaffe Fassett and Niki Turner, created a fascinating dreamland vision of the Forest of Arden.

APPENDIX I

Edith Evans' 1925 and 1936 Seasons with the Old Vic

1925 September to May First season at the Old Vic during Andrew Leigh's regime:

> *Portia in* The Merchant of Venice
>
> *Queen Margaret in* Richard III
>
> *Katherina in* The Taming of the Shrew
>
> *Mariana in* Measure for Measure
>
> *Cleopatra in* Antony and Cleopatra
>
> *The Angel in* The Child in Flanders *by Cecily Hamilton*
>
> *Mistress Page in* The Merry Wives of Windsor
>
> *Kate Hardcastle in* She Stoops to Conquer *by OliverGoldsmith*
>
> *Portia in* Julius Caesar
>
> *Rosalind in* As You Like It
>
> *Dame Margery Eyre in* The Shoemaker's Holiday *by Thomas Dekker*
>
> *The Nurse in* Romeo and Juliet
>
> *Beatrice in* Much Ado About Nothing
>
> Edith Evans' 1925 and 1936 Seasons with the Old Vic

1936 October to December   Returned once more to the Old Vic and played:

> Lady Fidget in The Country Wife by William Wycherley, Production by Tyrone Gutherie
>
> Rosalind in As You Like It production by Esme Church
>
> Mother Sawyer in The Witch of Edmonton by Dekker FordAnd Rowley, production by Michel Saint-Denis

APPENDIX II

Cast for the 1926 Production of <u>As You Like It</u> at the Old Vic

Director	Andrew Leigh
Duke	Allen Douglas
Frederick	Graveley Edwards
Amiens	Gerald Bonnin
Jacques	Balliol Halloway
Le Beau	Claude Ricks
Charles	Michael Watts
Oliver	Neil Porter
Orlando	Frank Vosper
Adam	John Garside
Touchstone	Duncan Yarrow
Corin	Horace Sequeria
Sylvius	John Wyse
William	William Monk
Hymen	Claude Ricks
Rosalind	Edith Evans
Celia	Nell Carter
Phebe	Amy Nowell
Audrey	Cicely Oates

APPENDIX III

Cast for <u>As You Like It</u> at The Old Vic in 1937

Director ....Esme Church

Scenery and Costume Designer............ Molly McArthur

Orlando ....Michael Redgrave

Adam...Andrew Churchman

Oliver ....Valentine Dyall

Charles ....Michael Brennan

Celia...Marie Ney

Rosalind ....Edith Evans

Touchstone ....Frederick Lloyd

LeVeau..Robert Eddison

Duke ....Harvey Baraban

Amiens ....Colin Cunningham

Corin..Frederick Bennett

Silvius..Robin Kempson

Jacques..Leon Quartermaine

Audrey..Freda Jackson

Phebe..Daphine Heard

William ....Robert Eddison

APPENDIX IV

Cast for the 1950 Production of As You Like It at the Cort Theatre in New York City

Director	Michael Benthall
Scenery and Costume Designer	James Bailey
Orlando	William Prince
Adam	Burton Mallory
Oliver	Ernest Graves
Dennis	Robert Foster
Charles	Michael Everett
Celia	Cloris Leachman
Rosalind	Katharine Hepburn
Touchstone	Bill Owen
Le Beau	Jay Robinson
Frederick	Dayton Lummis
Lady in Waiting	Jan Sherwood
Duke	Aubrey Mather
Amiens	Frank Rogier
Lord	Everett Gamnon
Corin	Whitford Kane
Silvius	Robert Quarry
Jacques	Ernest Thesiger

Phebe...Judy Parrish

Audrey...Patricia Englund

Sir Oliver Martext ....Jay Robinson

William ....Robert Foster

Rowland ....Craig Timberlake

APPENDIX V

Cast List for the Production of <u>As You Like It</u> for the Royal Shakespeare Company in 1961/62

Director...Michael Elliott

Scenery and costume Designs...............Richard Negri

Music..George Hall

Orlando...Ian Bannen

Adam..Clifford Rose

Oliver...David Buck

Dennis..Bruce McKenzie

Charles...Sebastian Breaks

Rosalind...Vanessa Redgrave

Celia...Rosalind Knight

Touchstone...Patrick Wymark

Le Beau..Ian Richardson

Frederick..Tony Church

Banished Duke....................................Paul Hardwick

Corin..Russell Hunter

Silvius..Peter Gill

Jacques...Max Adrien

Audrey...Patsy Byrne

Sir Oliver Martext...............................William Wallis

Phebe...Jeanne Heppel

William ....Richard Barr

Others: Gareth Morgan, Barry Stockwell, Michael Stephens, Eric
Flynn, James Kerry, Susan Engel, Narissa Knights, Rosemary Mussell,
Georgina Ward, Julian Battersby, Peter Holmes, Michael Murray,
Ronald Scott-Dodd, Michael Warchus, Brian Wright.

APPENDIX VI

List of Libraries and Centers for Performing Arts Research in the United States and England

Bermans and Nathans
Research Library
40 Camden Street
London NWI England

British Theatre Museum
Victoria and Albert Museum
South Kensington,
London, SW
(The Debenham bequest)
England

City of Philadelphia
Free Library
Theatre Collection
Logan Square
Philadelphia, Pennsylvania 19103

List of Libraries and Centers for Performing Arts Research in the United States and England

Harvard Theatre Collection
Harvard College Library
Cambridge, Massachusetts 02138

The Hon. Librarian
Vic-Wells Association
185 Honor Oaks Road
London, SE 23
England

Hulton Picture Library
Marytebone
High Street
London WI
England

The Illustrated London News
Picture Library
4 Bloomsburg Square
London WCIA 2RL
England

Library and Museum of the Performing Arts
The New York Public Library at Lincoln Center
111 Amsterdam Avenue
New York, New York 10023

Mander Mitchenson Museum
5 Venner Road
London, SE 26
England

Memorial Library
Royal Shakespeare Theatre Company
Stratford-on-Avon
Warwickshire

New York Theatre Critics Review
4 Park Avenue
Suite 21D
New York, New York 10016

The Old Vic Theatre
The Royal Victoria Hall Foundation
Waterloo Road
SE1 8NB
London
England

Smithsonian Institution
Information ad Research Center
51 Building, Great Hall
Washington, DC USA 20560

Theatre Guild Collection
Beinecke Rare Book and Manuscript Library
Yale University Library
1603 Yale Station
New Haven Connecticut 06526

APPENDIX VII

New Online Resources

Austin Film Society Stage History.
http://www.austinfilm.org/StudioStageHistory.php

France. National Library. http://www.bnf.fr/

Internet Research Studies for Shakespeare.
http://www.shakespeare.bham.ac.uk/resources/

Lawrence and Lee Theatre Research Institute. Ohio State University
USA. http://library.osu.edu/sites/tri/

Longman Anthology of Theatre.
http://www.actorschecklist.com/resources/international.html

Millennium stage The Kennedy Center Washington DC USA
http://www.kennedy-center.org/programs/millennium/history.html

National Center for the Performing Arts. Bombay, India.

Newberry Library. Chicago. USA
http://www.newberry.org/nl/newberryhome.html

Theatre Resources on the Web. University of Washington, USA.
http://www.videoccasions-nw.com/history/theatrer.html

Questia. Online Library.
http://www.questia.com/popularSearches/theater_history.jsp?CRI
D=nullCRnull&OFFID=am4t-th

UK Theatre Web. http://www.uktw.co.uk/

CHAPTER SIX

STAGE HISTORY EDUCATIONAL PARADIGM

Mastery in Teaching through Designing a Personal Project Overview for use of FINE ART define legacy of Katharine Hepburn. As example, I refer to my own recent scholarship in the field of education in the fine arts to further use of multiple intelligence theory in the college setting and change a limited paradigm that is in place now to a more fine art oriented paradigm that will free the human spirit and allow students to become within a setting that parallels Hepburn's education and fine art legacy.

My dissertation, which is in the collections of seven libraries in the United States, was a case study survey research experiment that I performed in 2003 to investigate the significant sustained performance of Northampton Community College students from January 2003 to December 2003. I used single post test only to study relationships of dependent variables to the use of modern songs with lyrics and their pedagogical application in the college English classroom. Ultimately I attempted to demonstrate a new framework for teaching college English through a combination of naturalistic observation and classification of variables. The subjects in the study were 70 students in two different sections of English I and three different sections of English II

The Importance of Stage History Synthesis and Transformation through Fine Arts in Education

Beginning   Art/Dance/Drama/Music/Writing as a Paradigm for Teaching Preschoolers

Verses   Art/Dance/Drama/Music/Writing a Paradigm for Teaching Elementary

Chorus   Art/Dance/Drama/Music/Writing as a Paradigm for Teaching Secondary

Bridge   Art/Dance/Drama/Music/Writing as a Paradigm for Teaching ESL

Lyrics   Art/Dance/Drama/Music/Writing as a Paradigm for Teaching College

Coda   Conclusions

The stage history thesis documented in this work demonstrates the importance of the stage as an historical reminder of our cultural heritage. In a sense, the histories of the performances of Rosalind depict a much larger view of how fine art of drama changes according to the society at large. As I record for future researchers and document production histories I also define a new era for students of fine arts to also look to history for curriculum and major study. As our culture of the new century focuses on different types of performances we need to look back on our past to understand the visions of our future in fine art. As Aristotle pointed out, art is imitation. We synthesize the fine arts to create ways of expressing our inner thoughts and emotions.

The Historiography section of my book investigates ways of applying theatre history as a viable curriculum K-graduate work.

Characters mirror stage history of century. A vital theatre/film industry reflects changes in the multicultural society it serves as do the performers. Katharine Hepburn acted as a female lead in most of her performances with the portrayal of a female being who affected audiences. Theatre as art form surpasses all other forms due to the nature and the scope of the effort that includes setting, language, characterization, mood, theme, and tone. The work of art of theatre or film brings to life a human moment. Preserved through our new technology, thankfully, we have films with Katharine Hepburn that date back as early as the 1930's. We have preserved in the archives of theatrical libraries research efforts to preserve theatre and the marvelous historical significance of all performances of merit. That was my initial impetus behind my thesis and my reason for writing this book.

Opening into a new paradigm for education: history of a culture determined through stage history. Stage history is a viable college major. I present a paradigm in this chapter for colleges to follow and theatre school as well. I promote that the student of stage history is as important as the actor who portrays the characters.

Plato determined that the spiritual exists in art and Aristotle taught art as imitation. I combine the two methods and also add Socratic innovation method of "know thyself" in journal discovery to promote fine art as a way of knowing inner knowledge that is transcendent and spiritual. Pairing dramatic art and music as well as writing in curriculums based on film study offers aesthetic dimension to education.

I present three separate curriculum designs in the follow chapter, two for college level and a suitable curriculum for K-12 as well.

Design I - College
Based on Study of Actor
Design II - College
Based on Study of Director
Design for K-12

Theatre is the character of a culture therefore insight into the historical vision of Katherine Hepburn's performances shows the nature of a society and values. The psychology of drama surpasses the other fine arts in its approach to the human psyche.

Design I - College

Based on Study of Actor
Semester I
Theatre History I
Semester II
Theatre History II
Semester III
Theatre History Independent Study
Semester IV
Theatre History Independent Study
Semester IV
Theatre History Practicum
Semester VI
Theatre History Practicum
Semester VII
Theatre History Practicum
Semester VIII
Theatre History Thesis

Design II – College
Based on Study of Director
Semester I
History of Directing Film
Semester II
History of Directing Theatre
Semester III
Directing Independent Study
Semester IV
Directing Practicum
Semester V
Directing Practicum
Semester VI
Directing Practicum
Semester VII

Directing Practicum

Semester VIII

Directing Thesis

The Importance of Stage History Synthesis and Transformation through Fine Arts in Education

Beginning   **Art/Dance/Drama/Music/Writing as a Paradigm for Teaching Preschoolers**

Even the most hardened child who has been through an abusive situation or a death in the family can benefit from a class that is based on fine art throughout the day. In fact, I developed a curriculum for troubled children that focuses on the use of art to enhance self-esteem through friendly companionship throughout the class with no restrictions on the child's inert inner self. In other words, in education, rather than use of a teacher directed class, we should employ a student directed class where the child is primary and learns through doing.

Verses   **Art/Dance/Drama/MusicWriting a Paradigm for Teaching Elementary**

The ideal classroom is a studio where the child can explore interests and try out their own mind as a process of learning. I suggest that children may research at an early age and produce writing and art focused projects that enhance their self esteem and allow them to work at their own pace.

Chorus   **Art/Dance/Drama/Music/Writing as a Paradigm for Teaching**

Secondary

The high school setting would be a place of learning and overwhelming peace with a focus on fine art learning activities that extend to community.

Bridge   **Art/Dance/Drama/Music/Writing as a Paradigm for Teaching ESL**

The students create the most humorous ways of seeing our culture and language. The community of ESL students could become friendly with our own middle school and high school students through programs that allow community involvement.

Lyrics   **Art/Dance/Drama/Music/Writing as a Paradigm for Teaching College**

Design III

I. SYNTHESIS

2	Beginning	FILM OF HEPBURN as a Paradigm for Teaching Preschoolers
3	Verses	FILM OF HEPBURN as a Paradigm for Teaching Elementary
4	Chorus	FILM OF HEPBURN as a Paradigm for Teaching Secondary
5	Bridge	FILM OF HEPBURN as a Paradigm for

Design for K-12

Pairing intelligences based on Multiple Intelligence Theory through the Fine Arts Enhances Reading and Writing Skills in All Curriculum Fields
All the world's a stage,
And all the men and women merely players:
They have their exits and their entrances;
And one man in his time plays many parts,
His acts being seven stages.

Coda   Conclusions

As part of a presentation for the Montgomery Community College Tenth Annual Technology and Learning Conference in the Philadelphia in 2004 October, I explored the results of my dissertation entitled Modern Music Transforms the College English Classroom. *I enhance this chapter with some data from that study since the research in the area of the fine arts in education is still mounting. In fact, Howard Gardner presented a paper entitled "Multiple Intelligences After Twenty Years" in 2003 at the American Educational Research Association in Chicago Illinois on April 21, 2003. He concludes that he is still trying to find a place for the arts in academic psychology (Gardner 1). Furthermore, he adds that as the Mozart Effect gains credibility he might rethink a relation between musical and special intelligences (Gardner 10). In my work here, I intend to suggest that fine art including music, art, dance, photography and theatre are directly related to the learning process of humans and should be incorporated in the educational programs for the masses.*

We are born to create. Fine art distributes vibrations of healing and stimulates nervous system into creative visualization that overcomes anxiety. Fine art flourishes human potential. Fine art education transforms lives through creativity. Theatre, visual arts, music, and dance in education produces results that surpass standard modes of education. *Most importantly, drama as a catalyst helps the student find a way to relate to the literary message and encode language through human characters in historical settings.*

The connection of fine art as representative of the culture of the student relates to the rhetoric found in the literary passages s/he reads. For example Katharine Hepburn's films hold cultural contextual meaning and metaphors. Students compare films to current multicultural literature and demonstrate connections. For example, the work of Sylvia Plath can be understood through the comparisons of her works to the works of Katharine Hepburn.

Fine art transforms and allows the student to learn literature, reading, and writing, through the theory that promotes coparticipation preceding knowledge (Bateson 1975). Fine art transforms the student's mind and prepares the student to learn. The participation in the selection of favorite drama, art, music by the student prepares the student to learn about literature, writing, and computer skills appropriate for writing and other curriculum subjects.

The paradigm for fine art as a method of teaching can be explored through various research projects that can be conducted in K-college classrooms. In fact, drama offers the educator the vast opportunities to develop children's minds to action for preparation for reading and other subjects. The paradigm will focus on fine art as the entry for the framework and proceed to integrate skills based on use of fine art to teach.

Initially, the teacher will have a background in one or more of the fine arts.

FINE ART *Contextual Framework*

1. Define Purpose of Lesson

2. Identify Transformational Qualities

3. List Transformational Goals

4. Fine Art Selection or Selections

5. Fine Art History Work or Works

6. Contextual Patterns of Fine Art

7. Annotation of Fine Art Work or Works

8. Metaphors in Context of Fine Art

9. Compare and Contrast Fine Art with Academic Subject

10. Context and Fine Art Applied to Research in a Personal Journal

11. Technology Interactions

13. Group
    Discussions
    Peer Critique

14. Project

15. Writing Process
    Brainstorming
    Clustering
    THESIS STATEMENT
    Outlining
    Drafting

16. CULTURE Student Gains Self Knowledge Evolution of Transformation

17. PRESENT Portfolio

CHAPTER SEVEN

MASTERY IN TEACHING THROUGH DESIGNING A PERSONAL PROJECT OVERVIEW FOR USE OF *HISTORIOGRAPHY*

Synthesis: HEPBURN THE PAINTER

Now, with the forthcoming auction of her estate at **Sotheby's New York**, a selection of some 100 paintings, sculptures, drawings and sketchbooks by Hepburn went on exhibition at the auction house June 3-10, 2004 and hit the auction block June 10-11, 2004. Hepburn is said to have made her first painting on **Howard Hughes'** yacht in 1938, and over the years completed more than 50 works, many of which depict scenes from her travels as well as views of the Los Angeles house she shared with **Spencer Tracy**.

I have discovered through a revisiting of an old thesis, the potential of historiography of Katharine Hepburn for educational purposes. For Chapter Seven, I have updated this work to include the possibility of a new historiography based on the growing legacy of the infamous Katharine Hepburn. I suggest that her legacy has just begun to change our cultural views of woman and education. I produce here activities and goals for educators ad families to use the legacy of this special actress for improvement of lives. *FINE ART TRANSFORMS curriculum designs*

Teaching All Subjects through Fine Art

Use Katharine Hepburn's Films to Teach History, Writing, Social Studies, Design.

Use the spaces provided to design a personal curriculum based on historiography of the films of Hepburn. Activities include watching the films, finding resources, writing projects, film projects based on the historiography of Hepburn's life work.

"A Bill of Divorcement" (1932)

"Christopher Strong" (1933)

"Little Women" (1933)

"Morning Glory" (1933) (Oscar, best actress)

"Break of Hearts" (1934)

"The Little Minister" (1934)

"Spitfire" (1934)

"Alice Adams" (1935) (Oscar nomination, best actress)

"Sylvia Scarlett" (1935)

"Mary of Scotland" (1936)

"A Woman Rebels" (1936)

"Quality Street" (1937)

"Stage Door" (1937)

"Bringing Up Baby" (1938)

"Holiday" (1938)

"The Philadelphia Story" (1940) (Oscar nomination, best actress)

"Keeper of the Flame" (1942)

"Woman of the Year" (1942) (Oscar nomination, best actress)

"Stage Door Canteen" (1943)

"Dragon Seed" (1944)

"Without Love" (1945)

"Undercurrent" (1946)

"The Sea of Grass" (1947)

"Song of Love" (1947)

"State of the Union" (1948)

"The African Queen" (1951) (Oscar nomination, best actress)

"Pat and Mike" (1952)

"Summertime" (1955) (Oscar nomination, best actress)

"The Iron Petticoat" (1956)

"The Rainmaker" (1956) (Oscar nomination, best actress)

"Desk Set" (1957)

"Suddenly, Last Summer" (1959) (Oscar nomination, best actress)

"Long Day's Journey Into Night" (1962) (Oscar nomination, best actress)

"Guess Who's Coming to Dinner" (1967) (Oscar, best actress)

"The Lion in Winter" (1968) (Oscar, best actress)

"The Madwoman of Chaillot" (1969)

"The Trojan Women" (1971)

"A Delicate Balance" (1973)

"The Glass Menagerie" (1973)

"Love Among the Ruins" (1975)

"Rooster Cogburn" (1975)

"Olly, Olly, Oxen Free" (1978)

"The Corn Is Green" (1979)

"On Golden Pond" (1981) (Oscar, best actress)

"George Stevens: A Filmmaker's Journey" (1984)

"Grace Quigley" (1984)

"Mrs. Delafield Wants to Marry" (1986)

"Laura Lansing Slept Here" (1988)

"The Man Upstairs" (1992)

"This Can't Be Love" (1994)

"Love Affair" (1994)

"One Christmas" (1994)

NOTES

Other scholars who are participating in the effort to promote MI Theory in education include Kathleen Gaffney, winner of the first ever U.S. Department of Education's "John Stanford Education Heroes Award" and president Artsgenesis in New York.

http://www.artsgenesis.com/history.html

> Lists of online stage history opportunities for scholars with dated format, new online resources current for researchers and scholars as well as students of stage history. Writing opportunities for students extend beyond the classroom to a network of historiography conferences both at location and online.

American Society for Theatre Research. Online. Available. Date of Access September 14, 2004.

http://library.trinity.wa.edu.au/subjects/english/drama/theatrehist.htm

Artsgenesis. Online. Available. Access Date September 14, 2004.

http://www.artsgenesis.com/history.html

As You Like It Online Version. Online. Available. Access date September 14, 2004.

http://the-tech.mit.edu/Shakespeare/asyoulikeit/

Brandeis University Theatre History Library Online. Online. Available. Access Date September 14, 2004.

http://library.brandeis.edu/resources/guides/theaterhistory.html

Collins Library University of Puget Sound Theatre History Research and Timeline. Online. Available. Access Date September 14, 2004.

http://library.ups.edu/instruct/ricig/theatre371/

The Complete Works of Shakespeare. Online. Available. Access Date August 9, 2004. Operated by The Tech. MIT's Oldest and Largest Newspaper.
  http://the-tech.mit.edu/Shakespeare/works.html

ENotes. William Shakespeare. Online. Available. Access Date August 9, 2004.
  ENOTES.com LLC http://www.shakespeare.com/

Gray, Terry. Mr. William Shakespeare on the Internet. Online. Available. Access date August 9, 2004.
  http://www.shakespeare.com/

Harvard Theatre Collection. Online. Available Date of Access September 14, 2004.
  http://hcl.harvard.edu/houghton/departments/htc/theatre.html

International Federation for Theatre Research. Online. Available. Date of Access September 14.
  http://www.firt-iftr.org/firt/home.jsp

Kingston Theatre on 24-26 High Street in Kingston upon Thames Surrey KT1 1HL United Kingdom. Online Available. Date of Access September 14, 2004.
  http://www.kingston.ac.uk/~kx19709/

Performance Arts Links. Online. Available. Date of Access September 14, 2004.
  http://www.theatrelibrary.org/links/ActorsHistory.html

Talkin' Broadway. Online. Available. Date of Access September 14, 2004.
  http://www.talkinbroadway.com/bway101/2.html

Theatre History Online Archives of Trinity College Australia. Online. Available. Access date September 14, 2004.

http://library.trinity.wa.edu.au/subjects/english/drama/
theatrehist.htm

And one man in his time plays many parts,
His acts being seven stages.

EPILOGUE

The importance of Katharine Hepburn's legacy to our cultural heritage is apparent at the time of this writing. In an Interview with Martin Scorsese by Rebecca Murray about his film <u>The Aviator</u> the director comments that he needed "an actress of great intelligence and courage" to play Katharine Hepburn in the film. We discussed levels of accent. When she came she said, "Look, I looked at some pictures of Katharine Hepburn and there's a couple here." And she got in a certain position sort of on her haunches, Cate Blanchett did, and she said, "I think she was like this." Sure enough, that's the way she's sitting on the beach when Howard comes up and asks her to go golfing with him. That was taken from a PR still off the set. And she just had It. She had the gesture, she had the lines to be, the body lines, the look of Katharine Hepburn.

All in all, I am thankful for the chance to share the method of writing I have learned with others. Often we as writers think we have to create a totally original work that we think of as lone artists. In fact, this is not the case. We are imitators, as Aristotle said of us. It is my hope that we all imitate the great Katharine Hepburn and make fine art our ways of lives in our future generations. I also thank Frank's wife Mary Jane Hook who was the Dean of the Northampton Community College when I taught drama to seniors and children in the 70's Mary Jane was aware of my extreme love of drama as a way of life for children and a way of education.

A study of past heroines such as Katharine Hepburn leads us to

89

design new ways of living or education. Hepburn's devotion to the study of performing art as a way of life is captivating and transcends time to produce a new vision for our future. Multi arts education will enhance our children's lives and enrich our schools. Based on my real life educational experiences, I proclaim a new paradigm for education with fine arts as the focus to teach reading, writing and mathematics as well as science and history.

A close study of Katherine Hepburn's characters on film the legacy we have to watch over and over again, overwhelm us with moral statements and bridge the gap between the twentieth and the twenty-first century visions of feminism. The legacy of the late Katharine Hepburn undeniably benefits a twenty-first century audience, because Kate identifies the artistic spirit that spans societal limitations and cultural attributes. As one of the most important women of the twentieth century, Hepburn was an artist who exemplified the independent character, freedom and opportunity available to women as paramount whether she was on stage or in film. As the late Hepburn, she has become a living art spirit with a legacy that acts as a shining example for women in the twenty-first century.

I have found significant data in this rebirth of an old study. I am not the same person I was when I wrote the original study. Through the journey of childbirth, career, searching for answers to life's dilemma's such as why we have to die and why we select certain ways to believe and perform faith, I have learned to cope through theatre. Historical and cultural affectations have motivated me to become what I am. In fact, her career offers a message of hope for the reader. Within her roles lie answers to life's decidedly hardest questions. For example, after reviewing the The Little Minister (1934) my sensibilities initiated excitement to be a woman of this era rather than the crude time period of the film. Hepburn portrays a gypsy character full of enthusiasm and joy. Nest, in the Sixties, Guess Who's Coming to Dinner (1967) holds lines that are inevitably grand for my own son as well as my college students. Hepburn plays a wife and mother with her extraordinary dignified characterization. On Golden Pond (1981) congratulates my sense of growing old with dignity and fortitude. In that film, Hepburn ages gently and advances peace and calmness for aging audiences. Movie therapy via the works of Hepburn effectively change a viewer. Assuredly, Hepburn's legacy delivers hope within the historical study of her characterizations on stage and film.

In Katharine Hepburn's autobiographical work entitled <u>Me, Stories of My Life</u>, she recounts how she was delighted with the performance at the Cort Theatre and calls the production "beautiful." Her ability to transcend the critiques and opinions of others is truly a grand legacy that shall resound in the hearts of all the young who attempt to find career, especially in the fine arts. She also says that she "learned a lot" by performing in Shakespeare. Another part of her legacy is her spirit of willingness to learn no matter what age and a delight in trying out new opportunities. As I walked the streets of New York City on January 1, 2005, I pondered the legacy. Thank you, Katharine.

GLOSSARY

antagonist – designates the character in a play who opposes the protagonist or hero

apron – that part of the stage which extends beyond the proscenium arch and the front curtain; sometimes called the fore stage

arc light – an especially intense and concentrated light source formed by passing an electric current between two rods of carbon; used first at the Paris Opera by M.J. Duboseq in 1846

backcloth – the flat, painted canvas used generally with a wing-flat et to cover the area at the back of the scene; usually hung from the grid

backing flat – a canvas-covered frame which painted and set behind openings in the stage set to conceal the area beyond it

backstage – all the areas behind the scene set on stage, including wings, dressing rooms

balcony – seating area above the ground floor or orchestra batten – a pipe or rod suspended from the grid upon which can be hung lights or scenery

border – a narrow strip of painted canvas which is fastened at the top edge only to a batten to hide the top of the stage as seen from the auditorium

box set – arrangement of flats on the stage forming three walls with a ceiling overhead

brace – an extensible wooden stick used in a diagonal position to support flats on stage

capa y estapa – "cloak and sword" play founded upon intrigues, mistaken identities, and so forth

catwalk – a narrow bridge suspended from the grid to enable stage hands to reach various parts of the scenery and lighting hung in the flies above stage

ceiling – canvas-covered frame usually hinged to fold in half, used to cover the top of a boxed set

cellar – area below the stage area, usually housing machinery employed for changing sets

chorus – in Greek Drama, the performers who sang and danced in the orchestra; now more generally applied only to groups who sing, although a group of performers who dance in musical plays is referred to as a chorus chronicle play – term applied, especially in England, two plays based on historical events, such as those of Shakespeare on English kings

Comedias – three-act plays on secular subjects

Comedia dell'arte – comedy which originated in the Italian Renaissance, largely improvised, using stock character and masks curtain – fabric hung in folds in the proscenium opening to hide the stage from the audience; also often used to indicate the end of a performance in phrases such as "at the final curtain"

cycle play – a series of Biblical plays originating in the Middle Ages

cycloramas – a curved canvas drop around the sides and back of the stage which is painted to look like sky, and which allows for the use of flies dimmer – a mechanical devise which allows for varying intensities of light to be used on stage dance the choreographer works with three basic elements: space, time and intensity.

director – supervisor for the preparation of the actors in their parts; responsible for the unity of the production through consultation with designers and other theatrical workers

downstage – portion of the stage area closest to the audience

drop – piece of scenery usually painted canvas, suspended from a batten and having no stiles at the side, but with a rail top and bottom

epilogue – a speech, usually in verse, given by one of the actors after the conclusion

farce – type of comedy with the emphasis upon situation rather than character

festoon drape – front curtain which is raised by drawing up particular parts to different heights to form a frame for the stage

Fine art – visual art, theatrical art, dance, music, writing, film and photography tell a story, reveal character or truth and illustrate ideas.

flat – a canvas-covered frame, usually rectangular in shape and painted, used in multiples for setting the scene on stage

flies – area above the stage, out of view of the audience, where scenery may be stored or lifted from the stage area

follow spot – concentrated beam of light operated so that it will constantly frame a particular performer as the character moves about the stage

footlights – strips of light in the floor at the edge of the stage apron

forestage – apron

front of house – all areas of the theatre ordinarily assigned to the audience, as distinguished from backstage

gallery – seating area placed nearest the roof in a theatre and thus farthest from the stage, containing the least expensive seats

gauze – device used for special effect; this drop of scrim cloth appears opaque when lit from the front but transparent when lit from behind

green room – the social room for performers behind the scenes; probably so called because it was usually painted green

grid – open framework above the stage from which battens and so forth are suspended

grooves – tracks on the stage floor and overhead upon which wings flats are moved

ground row – a long, low piece of scenery used across the bottom of the stage to hide lighting equipment

hand props – small, necessary objects carried on or off the stage by actors

ingenue – stage role of a young woman, usually naive

inner stage – portion of the area at the back of the stage which can be cut off from the rest by curtails or flats and can be revealed for a change of locale

inset – small scene set behind an opening in a larger scene

interlude – short dramatic sketch

kabuki – Japanese theatre emphasizing violent action and using more scenery than classic Japanese theatre

limelight – developed in the nineteenth century, intense illumination produced by heating a cylinder of lime to incandescence with gas; a position of prominence occupied by a performer

lines – words assigned to a particular actor mask, masque – a face covering; a presentation stressing spectacle and music

melodrama – type of drama stressing a succession of improbable incidents with one dimensional characters the method – an American term for a system of acting based on the teachings of Stanislavsky

mime – type of theatrical entertainment in Roman times consisting of short dramatic sketches with buffoonery and jesting

miracle play – medieval plays concerned chiefly with the lives of saints

morality play – didactic play with allegorical characters

multiple setting – type of setting where more than one locality is represented on stage at the time; "simultaneous setting"

mystery play – a cycle play with Biblical subject matter

naturalism – a literary movement of the late nineteenth century which stressed the presentations of persons and objects as nearly as possible in their ordinary, everyday forms

off stage – beyond the limits of the visible set on stage

on stage – a position in view of the audience

orchestra – the dancing circle for the chorus in classic theatre; the ground floor of a theatre

ozones – strips of blue cloth hung from battens and used for sky in stage settings

pageant – in Medieval England, the wagon on which the plays of the cycles were presented

pantomime – in Roman times, a type of theatrical presentation in which a chorus sang and actors mimed tragedies and love stories; today, a type of stage presentation with elaborate sets and music with no speaking parts

pastoral – theatrical presentation giving idyllic and artificial representation of country life

pit – ground floor standing room area

platform stage – a stage arrangement with the acting area not behind the proscenium arch as in Elizabethan theatre

producer – in England the person responsible for the staging of a play; in America, the individual who raises the money for production and oversees all details both artistic and financial

prologue – an introductory speech given at the beginning of the play, which calls attention to the theme of the play

prompt – supply an actor with his line

prompter – one who holds the play script and prompts

property room – storage space for stage props

props – objects on stage exclusive of scenery

proscenium – "before the scene" – the frame or arch which encloses the stage area

protagonist – the leading character in a play

rake – the slope of the stage floor upward from the audience

rail – the piece of wood forming the top or bottom of a flat

rehearsal – the preparation and practice of an acting group to prepare for the presentation of the play in front of an audience

relieve – a set in three dimensions

revolving stage – large turntable in the center of the stage which varying number of sets are placed

repertory – type of theatrical organization which has several plays ready to present

satire – type of drama which exposes, then scorns or ridicules human follies with the purpose of correcting these

scene – the stage setting; the division of a play or the act of a play; the locale where the action takes place

set – the scenery and properties for an act or scene; the act of putting the

scenery in place on the stage

set piece – any piece of scenery standing by itself in the scene

shadow show – puppets lighted from behind which cast shadows on a screen or cloth hanging between them and the audience

sill iron – flat medal pieces used across the bottom of openings in flats to add strength

stage door – entrance from the outside to the onstage areas

stiles – wooden strips which form the sides of a flat

stock company – company of actors who present plays in sequence at stated intervals

stock set – a standard stage set used in more than one play

subplot – a secondary line of action in a play

super – "supernumerary"; a performer who has a small part with no lines to speak

theatrical art – the most objective of the arts, since characteristically it presents both outer and inner experience through speech and action.

throwline – the cord used to tie flats together to form a wall, as in a box set

tormentor – curtains or flats at the sides of the stage behind the proscenium, forming an inner frame for the stage

trap — opening in the stage floor or walls of the scene which can be closed trilogy — series of three plays, usually on a single theme or a single story line

upstage — in a direction away from the audience

wagon stage — low flat platforms mounted on roller, each carrying a portion of the set, rolled on from the wings to form a complete set

wings — offstage areas to either side of the stage

wing flat — a flat at the side of the stage parallel to the footlights or the edge of the stage

THEATRE ARTS INTEGRATION IN THE LANGUAGE ALTERNATIVE SETTING IMPROVES AUTHENTIC STUDENT VOICE

How can teachers in elementary, secondary and college educational settings including real time, virtual and hybrid classrooms for multiple age groups manipulate the role of actor, director, set designer, producer, performer, script writer, and costume designer to enhance student voice? The answer lies in the truth that all teachers function as theatrical designers in roles who perform before their students. Applications of theatre art such as methods of acting, directorial applications, reader's theatre, staging plays and writing plays through teacher initiated or student created videos, powerpoints, chats, online conferences such as video conferences, and narrated power points mixed with and included in assignments, activities, and requirements delight students and help them learn to succeed even if they have never had an online class. In addition, a study of past heroes such as Katharine Hepburn leads educators to design new curriculum strategies for educational paradigms. Hepburn's legacy, a devotion to theatre art as a way of life, offers a captivating and transcending vision for our students in the virtual setting. Ultimately, theatre arts in the language alternative setting improves students' abilities to find their own voices.

The first method to use is the design of a framework entitled the Theatre Arts Integration Framework, designed to strengthen the teacher's performance and directorial function in the class situation in all classrooms.

Next, the teacher fits such paradigms as author impersonation into a rubric to implement student activities. Be current and use techniques that are fresh and strong in classrooms and that mirror current films. For example, elementary teachers direct, act, and perform as well as produce theatrically designed classes to teach respect for other's points of view or inner voice. Children especially need respect and space to create for all subjects. For instance in the art classroom teachers may create a day for pretending to be directors of movies. The children will write, direct, and perform their scripts to show their inner voices. The project can take up to six months and can allow teachers focus and excite students. A student group might focus on a time period such as Elizabethan England for a design theatrical period to learn to write, speak, and perform with classmates.

Characters mirror stage history of a century. A vital theatre/film industry reflects changes in the multicultural society it serves as do the performers. Katharine Hepburn acted as a female lead in most of her performances with the portrayal of a female being who affected audiences. Theatre as art form surpasses all other forms due to the nature and the scope of the effort that includes setting, language, characterization, mood, theme, and tone. The work of art of theatre or film brings to life a human moment. Preserved through our new technology, thankfully, we have films with Katharine Hepburn that date back as early as the 1930's. We have preserved in the archives of theatrical libraries research efforts to preserve theatre and the marvelous historical significance of all performances of merit.

Writing students can transform into stage historians; the possibilities for curriculum designs flourish within combination of theatre, society, actor, and audience. Theatre forms a culture. Plato determined that the spiritual exists in art and Aristotle taught art as imitation. Socratic innovation method of "know thyself" in journal discovery to promote fine art as a way of knowing inner knowledge is transcendent and spiritual. Pairing dramatic art and literature in writing curriculums based on film study offers aesthetic dimension to education.

Writers select a certain syntax to represent voice. Essentially, we are developing writing ability through finding personal writer voice meaning students' styles, contents, and formats. Student writers may use the live chat to act out a play or any work of literature with the use of reader's theatre. They can initiate the theatrical atmosphere by selecting a director for the chat, actors, script and performance date all of which may become a finished paper to present for a graded assignment. They might also create a video and critique their performances. Voice creates thesis. Hearing their own voices through theatrical means in virtual classrooms creates a doorway to learning to write.

According to Deconstruction Theory, language is metaphor. "Deconstruction assumes that since the word that signifies an object is separate from that object, the word stands for the object in a metaphorical way, and so all language is metaphorical " (Bogarad and Schmidt, 2002, p. 1353). Additionally, Reader Response Theory is the understanding that literary texts "must be understood rhetorically...for the effect they have on an audience...The emphasis is on understanding the text as a site where readers may produce meaning....Therefore, interpretation of a work is based on the reader's subjective response to it"(Bogarad and Schmidt, 2002, p. 1357).

Another literary theory, New Historicism supports "reading a literary work through its historical and social connect. The new historicist seeks to reconnect the text with the complexity of lived experience during its own time...The new historicist considers popular entertainment in relation to literary text equally important as representations of social reality" (Bogarad and Schmidt, 2002, p. 1363).

The emphasis on journaling, group activity, electronic portfolio, and electronic learning via theatre arts in writing classes are listed in current literary theories as new techniques for teaching writing. Mary Jo Potts suggests that "students who read widely and well tend to develop greater personal style and power as writers from their reading models...their writing skills rarely evolve without guidance and encouragement."

Her theories center upon helping students become effective writers through articulated departmental expectations, varying assignments with journals, teaching writing process, encourage developing style, and holistic scoring.

Furthermore, the Romantic Planning Framework designed by Kieran Egan (Kane, 1999), New Historicism, Reader Response Theory, Process Theory, Deconstructionism, Integrated Curriculum and Thematic Curriculum transform the virtual classroom situation and make the students relax so they could participate. "Some learners feel less threatened, which in turn lowers the affective filter or mental barrier that is 'caused by low motivation, high student anxiety, low student self-esteem' (Krashen, 1989, p. 10).

Journaling, writing process theory, electronic portfolio and team activities as well as methodology through the theatre art improves performances of students.

Curriculum Models

Integrated and/or Thematic Curriculum

According to David Sorbel (1999), "integrated curriculum strives to contextualize learning, to encourage children to see the connections between home life and school learning...to place the notion of authentic curriculum within the current context of holistic education...{which} recognizes the spiritual interests and pursuits of the child as a valid component" (Kane, 1999, p. 287-288). Therefore, *integrated* or thematic approach to curriculum advocates connections between curriculum and culture.

Read required literary works and establish means of understanding historical background, author biography, and alternative means of creativity of the work such as film or documentary on the writer. Film is a powerful tool in the understanding of literature. Students create their own primary sources such as interviews, reader's theatre on a chat type of group setting where we act out a virtual scene from a play as part of a team effort and experience to write about, a fiction or poetic work create by class members as an original primary document. The following list presents discussion teams and group collaborative efforts:

1. Creating a class glossary of dramatic terms that apply to

    literature

2. Creating a class list of quotations from famous actors, directors, literary figures as your discussions in a group of one or more

3. Creating links to web sites on literature and evaluating those links based on stage history

4. Haiku Book based on reader's theatre performances

5. Reader's Theatre via Chat Forum

6. Interview with family or co-worker about reaction to films

7. Designing a website

8. Designing a power point

9. Creating a power point for blackboard site that can be shared with the class

10. Creating a document that can be shared with others in a small group

JOURNALING

Self discovery is also a part of college learning and the art of theatre. A method of acting called the Stanislavsky Method offers the student insight into being or becoming the character. Students can write a stream of consciousness journal similar to a theatre production booklet for an actor. They can learn that a class is actually a production and the daily activities can mirror the practice needed for a play performance. Alternatively, a study of the inner consciousness of a student in a private journal is an alternative to show students how to write as well as a public discussion journal. A journal is a reflective writing that can be in sentence, poetry, or song lyrics that the student writes or even electronic in nature like a website or CD. Literary study can also engage students to write on issues that might be for Professor but not for other students. Journal entries often help writers create papers. Students are encouraged post paper drafts, develop papers, find research database articles or books, and provide responses for points toward class participation grade. Relate required readings to paper topics, current events, or life events as well.

Sample student journal entry:

"...*There is nothing more exhilarating than getting totally engulfed in a ... a good movie. You almost feel like you are there, feeling what the main character is experiencing.... It seems as if all of the most exciting books eventually get turned into a movie, and it almost seems as if it is every author's goal to get their book turned into a movie.*

The Romantic Planning Framework

First, the instructor identifies transcendent qualities. Next, s/he organizes the topic into narrative structure, then composes the body of the lesson and humanizes the content and pursues the details. Finally, the instructor concludes the topic and evaluates the content to see if s/he has engaged the students' imaginations (Kane, 1999, p. 311).

Literary Theories

New Historicism

New Historicism "represents a variant of sociological criticism. By reading a literary work through its historical and social context, the new historicist seeks to reconnect the text with the complexity of lived experience during its own time"

(Bogarad and Schmidt, 2002, p. 1363).   The participants design projects as well as class discussions, research papers and group activities based on their own views of creators of a new history about their own cultures based on theatre art.

Reader Response Theory

Reader response theory "emphasizes understanding the text as a site where readers may produce meaning" (Bogarad and Schmidt, 2002, p. 1357).

Deconstructionism

Deconstructionism determines that " language is metaphorical" (Bogarad and Schmidt, 2002, p. 1353).   Theatre art in the distance setting offers the instructor exciting motivational opportunities such as reader's theatre over a chat or video.

Methodology Examples Based on Theatre Arts

1. Team members create a video of their essays related to theatricality and the meaning of the performance in their own life situations.

2. Students create hyperlinks and review selections for papers and discussions. Many students design websites or web pages or essays based on web site review.

3. Design hypertext which is a combination of essay and links as well as documents from the internet to detail a presentation. Submit hypertext projects via a student generated film with director, actor, and story board.

4. Establish a team of student friends at the early stages of the class; work in teams of two or more to write and present

papers via alternative means like chat presentations, book poetry or drama talks with analysis of historical, biographical, and language analysis of literary works or group papers that give all students the same points for discussions drafts and final papers. Students enjoy cut and paste essay technique during chat sessions that can be copied and pasted for the entire class to view.

5. Power point presentations are possible and can be uploaded to virtual classrooms to satisfy essay. Incorporate the essay into the presentation. New technologies like flash and power point provide interesting technology to fit the essay structure and incorporate hypertext and hyperlinks as well.

6. Combine technologies and add video that can be mailed to Professor in groups of one or more on essays to present creations that animate and analyze.

7. Interview, provide a real time reader's theatre for an early childhood class or elderly care unit where you read literature and gain feedback, or create your own unique interview or field study for project. Field study can provide a link to essay structure and presentation.

8. Use stream of consciousness journaling as a set of papers. Journal with hypertext to present logical study of literary works and request presentations that show ability to journal and to document journal experience for alternative paper essays that can be submitted to publishers. Journaling and internet are powerful tools for English students.

9. Coffee House presentations can be done via the internet through chat or AOL instant messenger for class presentations that show group dynamics and understanding of the process of writing.

Furthermore, theatre arts combined in filmography study change the cultural view of the emerging writer in English classes and excites the imagination to produce student virtual writers who use hyperlinks, hypertext, and a combination of strategies to succeed. Educational frameworks enhance virtual platforms and focus the student on the use of the past to create a new history via reader response in literature computer based virtual classes.

The following passage from the conclusion of my master's thesis based on the study of stage history acts as a sample of the prose generated by use of fine art as a basis for virtual writing classes:

As a result of this investigative study, I have found that the role of Rosalind demands much from the actress. Rosalind has more sides and more puns than any other of Shakespeare's women. The role gives the actress a chance to achieve a modulation between the brassiness needed to enjoy being in disguise and the tenderness needed to portray love. Evans gave the most successful performance to Rosalind in the twentieth century. She discovered moments of sweetness that stage historians praise as moments which will never be forgotten. She transformed into Rosalind and portrayed her as the delightful comic heroine who captivates and entertains in the Forest of Arden (DiEdwardo).

Students will gain self knowledge as they learn to apply theatre arts applications such as acting, directing, and performing in the virtual setting. Grade achievement can be enhanced through theatricality in all aspects of curriculum design with author impersonation, reader's theatre chats, adding theatrical motives of forming text, hypertext, and hypermedia to consider how we as readers act, interact, and think visually with new and evolving forms and structures.

Works Cited

Berman, Jeffrey. (1994) B*erman Diaries to an English Professor: Pain and Growth in the Classroom.* Massachusetts: University of Massachusetts Press.

Bogarad, C.R. and Schmidt, J.Z. (2002) *Legacies*. New York: Harcour.

Bredendieck Fischer, Gwen. (1999) *Developing Students' Adaptive Learning Skills*. College Teaching. Vol.47, Issue 3.

DiEdwardo, MaryAnn Pasda. (2004) <u>Music Transforms the College English Classroom:</u>

<u>A Case</u> <u>Study.</u> Dissertation. California Coast University, Santa Ana, CA,

DiEdwardo, Maryann Pasda. (2005) "Pairing Music and Linguistic Intelligences." Kappa Delta Pi. <u>The Record</u>. Vol. 41, No. 3.

DiEdwardo Pasda, MaryAnn. (1980) <u>Rosalind in the Twentieth Century; An Analysis of</u>

<u>Performances</u> by Edith Evans, Katherine Hepburn and Vanessa Redgrave. Thesis. Bethlehem: Lehigh University.

Kane, Jeffrey. *(1999) Education, Information, and Transformation, Essays on Learning and Thinking*. New Jersey: Prentice Hall.

Kramer, Daniel J. (2001) ADFL Bulletin. "A Blueprint for Teaching Foreign LanguagesAnd Cultures through Music in the Classroom and on the Web."

Krashen, Stephen D. *(1989) Language Acquisition and Language Education. 2nd ed*. Language Teaching Methodology. New York: Prentice.

Potts, Mary Jo. (1998) *Teacher's Guide – AP English Language and Composition*. New York: College Entrance Examination Board and Educational Testing Service.

REFERENCES

Books

Addenbrooke, David. The <u>Royal Shakespearean Company: The Peter Hall Years.</u>

London: William Kimber, 1974.

Altman, George, Ralph Freud, Kenneth Macgowan, and William Melnitz. <u>Theatre</u>

<u>Pictorial.</u> Los Angeles: University of California Press, 1953.

Anderson, Peggy. <u>Great Quotes from Great Women.</u> New Jersey: Career Press, 1997.

Arnold, Janet. <u>A Handbook of Costume</u>. London: Macmillan, 1973.

Baker, Arthur E. <u>A Shakespeare Commentary</u>. New York: Ungar, 1964.

Barton, Lucy. <u>Historic Costume for the Stage</u>. Boston: Baker, 1963.

Bateson, Mary Catherine. "Mother-Infant Exchanges: The Epigenesis of Conversational Interaction." In D. Aaronson and R.W. Rieber (Eds.), <u>Developmental</u>

Psycholinguistic and Communication Disorders. Annals of the New York Academy of Sciences, *1975, 263, 101-113.*

Bateson, Mary Catherine. <u>Peripheral Visions, Learning Along the Way.</u> New York: Harper Collins, 1994.

Batters, Jean. <u>Edith Evans</u>. London: Hart-Davis MacGibbon, 1977.

Bertram, Joseph. <u>Acting Shakespeare</u>. New York: Theatre Arts Books, 1960.

Black, J. Anderson, and Madge Garland. <u>A History of Fashion</u>. New York: Greenberg, 1950.

Blum, Daniel. <u>A Pictorial History of the American Theatre</u>. New York: Greenberg, 1950.

----------------------. Theatre World: Season 1950-51. Vol. 7. New York: Greenberg, 1951.

Boleslavsky, Richard. <u>Acting: The First Six Lessons</u>. New York: Theatre Arts, 1933.

Bradby, G.F. <u>About Shakespeare and His Plays</u>. London: Oxford University Press, 1927.

Brown, Ivor<u>. Shakespeare and His Time. </u>Edinburgh: Nelson and Sons, 1960.

--------------. <u>Shakespeare and the Actors</u>. London: Bodley Head, 1970.

Brown, John Mason. <u>The Art of Playgoing</u>. New York: Norton, 1936.

----------------------. <u>Dramatis Persona</u>. New York: Viking Press, 1963.

Brown, John Russell. Shakespeare and His Comedies. London: Methuen, 1957.

------------------------------. Shakespeare's Plays in Performance. New York: St. Martin's Press, 1967.

------------------------------. Shakespeare and His Comedies. London: Methuen, 1968.

------------------------------. Shakespeare's Dramatic Style. New York: Barnes and Noble, 1971.

Burton, Hal, ed. Acting in the Sixties. London: British Broadcasting Company, 1970.

Camesasca, Ettore, and John Sunderland. The Complete Paintings of Watteau. New York: Abrams, 1968.

Campbell, Oscar James, and Edward G. Quinn, eds. A Shakespeare Encyclopedia. London: Methuen, 1966.

Carey, Gary. Katharine Hepburn, A Hollywood Yankee. New York: Pocket Books, 1975.

Clarke, Mary and Rodger Wood. Shakespeare at the Old Vic. London: Adam and Charles Black, 1956.

Crimp, Susan. Katharine Hepburn Once Said…Great Lines to Live By. New York: HarperEntertainment, 2003.

Crosse, Gordon. Fifty Years of Shakespearean Playgoing. London: Mowbray, 1941.

-----------------. Shakespearean Playgoing 1890 to 1952. London: Mowbray, 1953.

Dean, Alexander and Lawrence Cara. Fundamentals of Play Directing. New York: Holt, Rinehart and Winston, 1974.

DeBanke, Cecile. Shakespeare Stage Production Then and Now. London: Hutchinson, 1954.

Dickens, Homer. The Films of Katharine Hepburn. New York: Citadel Press, 1971.

Dunn, Esther Cloudman. Shakespeare in America. New York: Macmillan Company, 1939.

Edwards, Anne. Katharine Hepburn, A Remarkable Woman. New York: St. Martin's Griffin, 2000.

Ellis, Ruth. The Shakespeare Memorial Theatre. London: Winchester, 1948.

Evans, G. Glakemore, ed. The Riverside Shakespeare. Boston: Houghton-Mifflin, 1974.

Farjeon, Herbert. The Shakespearean Scene. London: Hutchinson, 1948.

Forbes, Bryan. Dame Edith Evans: Ned's Girl. Boston: Little, Brown, and Company, 1977.

Gardner, Helen. "As You Like It." In Shakespeare: The Comedies. Ed. Kenneth Muir. Englewood Cliffs: prentice Hall, 1965. pp. 58-71.

Gardner, Howard. Frames of Mind. New York: Basic Books, 1983.

Gardner, Howard. Multiple Intelligences. New York: Perseus Books, 1993.

Gassner, John, and Edward Quinn, eds. The Reader's Encyclopedia of World Drama. New York: Crowell, 1969.

Goodwin, John, ed. Royal Shakespeare Theatre Company 1960-1963. New York: Theatre Arts Books, 1964.

Hagen, Uta. Respect for Acting. New York: Macmillan, 1973.

Hainaux, Rene, ed. Stage Design Throughout the World Since 1935. New York: Theatre Arts Books, 1956.

Hapgood, Elizabeth Reynolds, trans. An Actor Prepares. By Constantine Stanislavsky. New York: Theatre Arts, 1936.

Hartnoll, Phyllis, ed. The Oxford Companion to the Theatre. London: Oxford University Press, 1951.

Hepburn, Katharine. The Making of African Queen or How I Went to Africa with Bogart, Bacall and Huston and Almost Lost My Mind. New York: Alfred A. Knopf, Inc., 1987.

Hepburn, Katharine. Me, Stories of My Life. New York: Knopf, Inc., 1991.

Higham, Charles. Kate, The Life of Katharine Hepburn. New York: Norton Press, 1975.

Howard, Diana. London Theatres and Music Halls 1850-1950. London: Library Association, 1970.

Hunt, Hugh. Old Vic Prefaces. London: Routledge and Kegan Paul, 1954.

Johnson, Hamish and Peter Quinnell. Who's Who in Shakespeare. New York: William Morrow, 1963.

Kanin, Garson. Tracy and Hepburn – An Intimate Memoir. New York: Bantam Books, 1972.

Kirschbaum, Leo. Character and Characterization in Shakespeare. Detroit: Wayne State University Press, 1962.

Laver, James. English Costume of the Eighteenth Century. London: A. and C. Black, 1931.

Mackenzie, Agnes Mure. The Women in Shakespeare's Plays. London: William Heinemann, 1924.

Maitra, Sitansu. Shakespeare's Comic Idea. Calcutta: Firma K.L. Mukhopadhyay, 1960.

Marill, Alvin H. Katharine Hepburn. New York: Pyramid, 1973.

Marshall, Norman. The Producer and the Play. London: Davis-Poynter, 1957.

Martz, William J. Shakespeare's Universe of Comedy. New York: David Lewis, 1971.

McGaw, Charles. Acting is Believing. New York: Holt, Rinehart and Winston, 1966.

Muir, Kenneth. "The Critic, the Director and Liberty of Interpreting." In The Triple Bond. Ed. Joseph G. Price. University Park: Pennsylvania State University Press, 1975.

Nathan, George Jean. The Theatre Book of the Year (1949-1950): A Record and Interpretation. New York: Alfred A. Knopf, 1950.

Nicoll, Allardyce. The Theatre and Dramatic Theory. Westport: Greenwood Press, 1962.

Oenslager, Donald. Stage Design: Four Centuries of Scenic Invention. New York: Viking Press, 1975.

Parker, K.T. The Drawings of Antoine Watteau. London: B.T. Batsford, 1931.

Parrott, Thomas Marc. Shakespearean Comedy. New York: Russell and Russell, 1962.

Phialas, Peter G. Shakespeare's Romantic Comedies. Chapel Hill: North Carolina Press, 1966.

Rosenfeld, Sybil. A Short History of Scene Design in Great Britain. Totowa: Rowman and Littlefield, 1973.

Salgado, Gamini. Eyewitnesses of Shakespeare (1590-1890). New York: Barnes and Noble, 1975.

Shakespeare, William. As You Like It. Cambridge: Cambridge University Press, 1926.

Spada, James. Hepburn, Her life in Pictures. New York: Doubleday ad Company, Inc., 1984.

Speaight, Robert. Shakespeare on the Stage. Boston: Little, Brown, and Company, 1973.

Spencer, Theodore. Shakespeare and the Nature of Man. New York: Macmillan, 1974.

Sprague, Arthur Colby. Shakespeare and the Actors: The Stage Business in His Plays (1660-1905). Cambridge: Harvard University Press, 1944.

------------------------. Shakespearean Players and Performances. Cambridge: Harvard University Press, 1953.

Sprague, Arthur Colby and J.C. Trewin. Shakespeare's Plays Today. Columbia: University of South Carolina Press, 1970.

Styan, J.L. The Shakespeare Revolution. Cambridge: Cambridge University Press, 1977.

Tillyard, E.M.W. The Elizabethan World Picture. New York: Vintage Books. Trewin, J.C. Edith Evans. London: Camelot, 1954.

------------. Shakespeare on the English Stage (1900-1964). London: Barrie and Rockliff, 1964.

-------------. Going to Shakespeare. Boston: Allen and Unwin, 1978.

Webster, Margaret. <u>Shakespeare Today</u>. London: J.M. Dent and Sons, 1957.

Dissertation

DiEdwardo, Mary Ann. "Music Transforms the College English Classroom." Diss. California Coast University, Santa Ana, California, 2004.

Paper

Gardner, Howard. "Multiple Intelligences After Twenty Years." Paper presented at the American Educational Research Association, Chicago, Illinois, April 21, 2003.

Articles

"As You Like It with Katharine Hepburn." <u>Theatre Arts Monthly</u>, 24, No. 4 (1950), p. 14.

Clark, Constance M. and Mary Elizabeth Devine. "The Stanislavski System as a Tool for Teaching Dramatic Literature." College English, 38, No. 1 (Sept. 1976), pp. 15-24.

DiEdwardo, Maryann Pasda. "Pairing Music and Linguistic Intelligences Develops Reading and Writing Skills." <u>The Record</u>, Spring 2005. Kappa Delta Pi, International Education Honors Society, member of the Alpha Alpha Chi Chapter.

Hyde, Mary Crapo. "Katharine Hepburn's As You Like It." <u>Shakespeare Quarterly</u>, 1, No. 2 (1950), pp. 54-55.

Recordings

Shakespeare, William<u>. As You Like It.</u> With Vanessa Redgrave, Ian Bannen, Rosalind Knight, Max Adrien and entire cast. Director Michael Elliott. Phonotape – Cassette. Caedman OCLC 002314, 1962.

Letters

Hepburn, Katharine. Letter to Author. 26 February 1980.

Sammassimo, Silvania. Secretary to Vanessa Redgrave. Letter to Author. 29 February 1980.

Online Resources

Albemarle of London. E and OE. Online. Available. Date of Access October 20, 2004.
   http://www.albemarle-london.com/rsc-asyoulikeit.html

Art New World Wide Corporation. ARTNET NEWS. Katharine Hepburn Secret Painter. 3-26-04. Date of Access October 10, 2004. Online Available. ArtNET .com
   http://www.artnet.com/Magazine/news/artnetnews2/
   artnetnews3-26-04.asp

Dirks, Tim. <u>Academy Award Winners and History</u>. "Katharine

Hepburn in Morning Glory." Online. Available. Date of Access October 21, 2004.

http://www.filmsite.org/morn.html

Murray, Rebecca. ABOUT. An Interview with Martin Scorese. ©2005 About, Inc. All rights reserved. A PRIMEDIA Company. http://romanticmovies.about.com/od/theaviator/a/aviatorms121004. htm

Reviews

"A Rosalind We Shall Always Remember." Review of Vanessa Redgrave's performance of Rosalind in 1961. Author identified as R.B.M. Located in files in Performing Arts Research Center, Lincoln Center, New York City.

"A Very Honest Actress." London Observer. 17 October 1976. Review of Edith Evans Success as an Actress.

"As You Like It." Review of 1937 Production found in Harvard Theatre Collection Catalogued under "Evans as Rosalind."

"As You Like It." Review of Edith Evans' Performance of Rosalind. London Times, 12 February 1937, Theatre Section, 12b.

"As You Like It." Review of Opening at Aldwych Theatre in January 1962. London Times, 11 January 1962.

Review of Vanessa Redgrave as Rosalind. "As You Like It Seen in England." New York Times, 5 June 1961, Sec. L, p. 30, col.1.

Review of Katharine Hepburn as Rosalind. "As You Like It." Theatre Arts Monthly, 34, no. 2 (1950), p. 14.

Atkinson, Brooks. "At the Theatre," New York Times, 27 January 1950, in New York

Theatre Critics Review, XI, No.2, 30 January 1950, p. 369.

Barnes, Howard. "Hepburn in Tights." Herald Tribune, 27 January 1950, in New York Theatre Critics Review, XI, No.2, 30 January 1950, p. 369.

Review of Miss Hepburn's Performance of Rosalind in New Haven, Connecticut in December 1949. Author identified a Bone, Legitimate, 8 December 1949, p. 60.

Brown, Ivor. "As You Like It." London Observer, Sunday 14 February 1937, Theatre Section.

Brown, John Mason. "That Forest of Arden." Saturday Review, February 1950, pp. 24 - 26.

Carroll, Sydney W. "The Art of Edith Evans, A Real Actress." London Observer, 1937.

Chapman, John. "Hepburn an Attractive Rosalind in Guild's Lovely As You Like It." Daily News, 27 January 1950, in New York Theatre Critics Review, XI, No.2, 30 January 1950, p. 369.

Coleman, Robert. "As You Like It at the Cort in Superb Production." Daily Mirror, 27January 1950, in New York Theatre Critics Review, XI, No.2, 30 January 1950, p. 367.

Garland, Robert. "Hepburn is Cheered for 'Rosalind Role'," American Journal, 26 January 1950, in New York Theatre Critics Review, XI, No.2, 30 January 1950, p. 368.

Heidt, Joseph. Press Release for The Theatre Guild. Review of Miss Hepburn's Performance of Rosalind in 1950. 23 West 53rd Street, New York 19, New York.

Lambert, J.W. "A Sunbeam in Arden." London Sunday Times, 9 July 1961.

---------------. "All For Our Delight." London Sunday Times, 14 January 1962. Review of Edith Evans' Performance of Rosalind. London Observer, 11 December 1936.

Morgan, Charles. "Of Drama by the Thames." London Observer, 11 December 1936. Review of Edith Evans' Performance of Rosalind. London Times, 12 February 1937, p.12, col. 2.

Review of Edith Evans' Performance of Rosalind in 1937. Play Pictorial, 1937, pp. 10-11.

Skolsky, Sidney. "Tintypes...Edith Evans." New York Post, 16 March 1968.

Tynan, Kenneth. Review of As You Like It production at Stratford-on-Avon in July 1961. Located in files of Performing Arts Research Center at Lincoln Center, New York City.

Wardle, Irving. "Another Part of the Forest." The London Observer, 14 January 1962.

Watts, Richard Jr. "Shakespeare Delightfully Done." New York Post, 27 Janaury 1950, in New York Theatre Critics Review, XI, No.2, 30 January 1950, p. 368.

"The Week's Theatre." Newspaper review of Edith Evans' performance of Rosalind in 1926, found in the files of the Harvard Theatre Collection, room 90, extension 5-2445 of the Harvard University Library.

Whittaker, Herbert. "Acting, Cooking in the Timing." New York Times, found in Performing Arts Research Library at Lincoln Center, filed under Edith Evans.

Educational Background

Doctorate of Education California Coast University 2004

Master of Arts in English   Lehigh University 1980 Sigma Tau Delta, Instructor, Scholarship, Stage History Thesis

Bachelor of Arts in Theatre Arts   Pennsylvania State University 1975 Summa Cum Laude, Carnegie Scholarship, Graduation Marshall College of Arts and Architecture, President of Mortar Board, Phi Beta Kappa, Phi Kappa Phi, Instructor for Penn State Lehigh Valley

Artist Trained in the United States of America, Maryann is primarily known as a landscape painter and a Shakespearean illustrator. Her works are in private collections and galleries in Europe and North America. Her landscape paintings are en plein air style (literally painting in the open air) compositions that evolve from abstract design to integrate design, color, proportions and balance, and to present poignant images or versions of reality edited by the artist. Maryann's landscapes are metaphors representing clarity of thought. Recent works include the 36"x 36"oil painting entitled Millbrook Marsh #1 for Joseph Pasda" for the permanent collection at Millbrook Marsh Environmental Center at Pennsylvania State University, Pennsylvania U.S.A.

Reviewer Distinguished Editorial Review Panel for Kappa Delta Pi International Honor Society in Education Indianapolis, Indiana, www.kdp.org **2005-present**

Pasda Art Studios Artist in Residence, Lecturer, Instructor 1975-present
Courses I teach include portfolio preparation, college preparation skills, drawing, painting, sculpture

College Lecturer, Adjunct Faculty, Guest Lecturer *I offer ongoing presentations on my research in education and specialize in teaching process theory, pre-writing, research and technology based writing to college level students*   *1980-present*

Himalayan Institute Lifetime Member, I.A.Y.T. International Association of Yoga Therapists

Global Classroom Management, Educational Leadership, Community Service, Curriculum Development, Publishing MaryAnn Pasda DiEdwardo Correspondence

Study www.maryannwriting.com www.maryannwriting.com/apcourses and www.
maryannwriting.com/books January 1993   (discontinued 2004) Courses K-adult
Writing, Advanced Placement MaryAnn Pasda DiEdwardo Publishing 94 curriculum
guides and educational publications

Awards and Professional Organizations

Woman of the Year 2006 American Biographical Institute,   Research Fellow
American Biographical Institute 2005, 2005 Woman of Achievement Award
American Biographical Institute, Outstanding Intellectuals of the 21st Century
International Biographical Center Cambridge Great Britain, Great Minds of the
21st Century, **Northampton Community College Project Aware Outstanding
Service Award 1978**, Kappa Delta Pi International Honor Society in Education,
Modern Language Association, Sedona Arts Center, Lifetime Member Himalayan
Institute, Who's Who in the World, Research Board of Advisors American
Biographical Institute, Lifetime Member Alumni Association Pennsylvania State
University and Lehigh University, The Haiku Society of America, Who's Who in
American Colleges and Universities, Who's Who in America, Who's Who Among
American Teachers, Outstanding Young Women of America, Honors International
Society of Poets, State Teaching Awards State of Pennsylvania Department of
Education Recycling and Archaeology Contests, Publishing Poynter Celebrity
Author Award for Write a Book of Haiku and Trees, Patron Member of New York
Academy of Sciences, Great Women of the 21st Century, lecturer for educational
conferences in the State of Pennsylvania, published award-winning poet for The
International Society of Poets and Educational Publications, Published Honorable
Mention Poet American Poetry Anthology; The National Library of Poetry

Thesis, Dissertation, Publications, Lectures, and Presentations
"Pairing Music and Linguistic Intelligences." Record, Vol. 41, No. 3, Spring
2005. Kappa Delta Pi, International Education Honors Society, member of the
Alpha Alpha Chi Chapter.

Thesis in archives Lehigh University Library
Pasda, MaryAnn. Rosalind in the Twentieth Century; An Analysis of
Performances by Edith Evans, Katharine Hepburn and Vanessa Redgrave. Thesis.
Bethlehem: Lehigh University, 1980.

Dissertation (Pennsylvania State University, Harvard University, Montgomery
Community College, Northampton Community College, DeSales University,
Lehigh University, California Coast University own manuscript hard copies)
DiEdwardo, MaryAnn Pasda. Music Transforms the College English Classroom:
A Case Study. Dissertation. California Coast University, Santa Ana, CA, 2004.

Presenter

"Pairing Linguistic and music Intelligences in Technology Enhanced and Distance Classrooms." Presenter for the Cedar Crest College Technology Symposium 2006 August

Lecturer for Montgomery County Community College Technology Conference 2004 October

Lecturer for Lehigh Carbon Community College Teaching Learning Center Lunch and Learn for Faculty Lecture and Video for Archives 2005

Power Point: MUSIC TRANSFORMS THE COLLEGE ENGLISH DISTANCE LEARNING CLASSROOM "Most importantly, music as a catalyst helps the student find a way to relate to the literary message and encode language through sound". Maryann Pasda DiEdwardo Ed.D.

Bethlehem Area Public Library Art Exhibit and Demonstration for the Public April 2006

Lecturer, Storytelling, Art Demonstration, Exhibit Barnes and Noble Booksellers Easton PA   Public Exhibition   October 2005

"Modern Music Transforms the College English Classroom and the Distance Learning Virtual Classroom" Copyright 2004 DiEdwardo

My Original Musicality Contextual Framework

12. Define Purpose of Lesson

13. Identify Transformational Qualities

14. List Transformational Goals

15. Music Selection or Selections

16. Literary Work or Works

17. Contextual Patterns of Music and Literature

18. Annotation of Song or Songs and Literary Work or Works

19. Metaphors in Context of Music and Literary Works

20. Compare and Contrast Music and Literature
21. Context and Music Applied to Research

22. Types of Prose

To Narrate
To Explain
To Describe
To Define
To Compare and Contrast
To Analyze
To Argue

23. Journal Discussions

24. Technology Interactions

14. Group
Discussions
Peer Critique
Project

15. Writing Process
Brainstorming
Clustering
THESIS STATEMENT
Outlining
Drafting

16. CULTURE Student Gains Self Knowledge Evolution of Transformation

17. PRESENT Portfolio

Teacher In-Service Courses and Consultations in Art   Allentown Diocese 1979-present

"Advanced Placement English Language and English Literature" for Pennsylvania Homeschoolers Annual Summer Conferences Harrisburg, PA 1998-2002.

Lecture Power Point <u>Kolbe Saint of the Immaculata</u>, Abundant Graces, 2002.

Poetry of Praise Power Point Presentation. DeSales University Library, 2002.

Haiku, Sumi-e, Origami Lecture Demonstration Program for Children and Adults Pocono Manor and Jacobsburg Environmental Centers   1997-2000

Lectures and Demonstrations Lehigh Valley Community, Northeastern PA and Pocono Area for Businesses, Private and Public Schools, 1977-present. Modified list follows: Borders Books and Music Café, Barnes and Noble, St. Ann's Elementary School, St. Jane's Elementary School, Holy Family School, Asa Packer Public Elementary School, Farmersville School, Sacred Heart School in Bath, Sacred Heart School in Miller Heights, Our Lady of Perpetual Help School, St. Simon and Jude School, Holy Infancy School, Holy Family School, Notre Dame of Bethlehem, St. Michael's School, St. Elizabeth's School, Bethlehem Christian School, City of Bethlehem Historic District, Moravian Academy of Bethlehem, Bethlehem Area Public Library, Pocono Manor Lecture and Demonstration

Co-authored original texts, international literary journal, and curriculum guides including the following:

DiEdwardo, MaryAnn and Patricia J. Pasda. <u>Write A Book Of Haiku.</u> Bethlehem. MaryAnn P. DiEdwardo Publishing, 1994.

DiEdwardo, MaryAnn Pasda and Patricia J. Pasda. <u>Paint a Book of Sumi-e.</u> Bethlehem: MaryAnn P. DiEdwardo Publishing, 2001.

DiEdwardo, MaryAnn Pasda and Patricia J. Pasda. <u>Trees.</u> Eared money to plant trees for Plant-It 2000, a global organization founded by the late John Denver. Bethlehem: MaryAnn P. DiEdwardo Publishing, 1999.

Educational Newsletters

1994-2001 - Articles in PA Newsletter about Homeschooling, Reading, Advanced Placement English including the following:

DiEdwardo, MaryAnn Pasda. Architecture in the Homeschool. Susan Richman, Ed. <u>Pennsylvania Homeschoolers International Newsletter</u>, Issue 46, Winter February 1994.

Printed in the United States
77867LV00003B/175-177